The Grateful Entrepreneur

40 GRATITUDE STRATEGIES TO BUILD RELATIONSHIPS, GROW YOUR BUSINESS AND MAKE MORE MONEY

SCOTT COLBY

The Grateful Entrepreneur: 40 Gratitude Strategies to Build Relationships, Grow Your Business and Make More Money

Publishing services provided by  **Archangel Ink**

ISBN-13: 978-1-7238-7031-6

What Others are Saying about
The Grateful Entrepreneur...

Scott Colby has 'hit the bulls-eye'—he understands the power of authentic gratitude in the context of business relationships. By applying the 40 practical tips he provides, leaders will be able to grow their business and customer loyalty at an incredible rate and to an extraordinary height. Do what he says, and you will be successful!

—Paul White, Ph.D., Co-author of the best seller, *5 Languages of Appreciation in the Workplace*

Scott Colby has written a book that successfully addresses the most overlooked secret for entrepreneurial success in the 21st century. If you are looking for the formula to transform your business from the inside-out, this book is for you.

—Pat Rigsby, Author of *The Ideal Business Formula*

Being an entrepreneur is hard. Really hard. Possibly the hardest thing you'll ever have to do in your life. And the one way you'll be able to keep moving forward is by being GRATEFUL. Now, Scott Colby has finally written THE book on this vital topic. Read it. Live it.

—Ryan Lee, Founder at Rewind

Scott Colby articulates the importance of "The Grateful Entrepreneur" in both life and business in such a powerful and unique way.

—Tony Grebmeier, Host of the *Be Fulfilled* podcast

Dedication

This book is dedicated to all the people of Guatemala who showed me what gratitude truly is.

I'm grateful

for you John

Scott Kelby

Contents

Introduction

It was July 14, 2014, when I stepped off the bus in Chonoxte, Guatemala. What I witnessed next took me by surprise.

There were two lines of people starting from the bus and stretching all the way back to the school. I saw people of all ages—kids, parents, and grandparents. It felt like the entire community of Chonoxte was there.

I arrived in Guatemala to help build schools with an organization called Hug It Forward.

Hug It Forward facilitates building classrooms using eco-bricks, which are plastic bottles stuffed with inorganic trash. During the project process, entire communities come together to build a more environmentally responsible educational space for their future.

As the other volunteers and I walked between the two lines of people, everyone smiled and clapped. They gave us high fives and hugs. Many villagers waved the American flag, and music blared from the sound system.

I felt like a famous rock star beloved by this entire community.

In reality, I was a stranger, some 2,398 miles from my home in Denver, Colorado.

Why did I feel more special and loved stepping off that bus in a remote village in Guatemala than I'd felt in all my years living in Denver?

Gratitude.

The community was showing their gratitude to the volunteers who had come for six days to help them build a school—a school they sorely needed.

Over the course of those six days, my eyes were opened to a new world. This community had so few material possessions.

No computers.

No TVs.

The newest iPhone? Forget about it! They didn't even have older iPhones—or any smartphones for that matter.

I discovered that convenience was not commonplace in Chonoxte. Sometimes families of ten to twelve people lived together in a run-down, single-room home.

Many villagers slept on the floor.

There was very little clean water and not much food.

The same was true of their school. At the time, it was a dilapidated one-room building shared by grades one through six.

This made for cramped, poor learning conditions.

But the one thing this village did have that showed up time and time again during my six days there were smiles. Happiness was abundant in Chonoxte.

And gratitude.

There's that word again.

The people of Chonoxte, though they had very little, were happy and appreciative for what they did have.

Which wasn't much.

How can that be? In the United States, we're constantly complaining about what we don't have.

Not having enough stuff.

Not having enough money.

Not having the latest smartphone.

We whine about the cold weather, the hot weather, the job we hate, the vacation we can't take, the house that's too small, and the fact that there's "nothing to eat in the fridge."

And the list goes on.

My time in Guatemala really shifted my perspective on life. And my encounter with gratitude didn't end there. When I returned home to Denver, I quickly recognized it had come home with me, like a stowaway in my luggage. Before I knew it, I was seeing the need for gratitude everywhere I looked. More than anything else, I was struck by its potential in my professional relationships.

I'd become overly sensitive to all the complaining we do in the United States, so I began learning about the positive benefits gratitude can have on people. Grateful people have more joy, happiness, and optimism. I decided I wanted to create a gratitude movement called Say It With Gratitude.

I've been a big believer in handwritten thank you notes from an early age, when my parents made me send cards to Grandma and Grandpa to thank them for Christmas presents. So I decided to start my gratitude movement with thank you cards.

What a powerful way to make people feel good and put a smile on their face—by sending out handwritten thank you notes!

Wanting to get kids and charities involved in my new venture, I decided to have kids draw the artwork for the cards! Say It With Gratitude's first set of cards were drawn by kids from Guatemala, and a portion of sales were donated to Pencils of Promise, another organization that builds schools in Guatemala and other developing countries.

How's that for a circle of good?

So what does that have to do with businesses?

As a customer, you want to feel valued; you want to be treated like a person. When that happens, you tend to be loyal to a company.

But this rarely happens anymore.

Companies don't send cards in the mail. Baristas don't greet you when you walk into a coffee shop. The sales-person ignores you when you step into the clothing store. Nobody says hello to you. No one learns your name or anything about you.

How many times have you sat down at a restaurant, but the server never shows up?

How many times have you been put on hold by a business for what seems like forever?

You feel like a number. Like a nuisance.

If that's how a business makes you feel, why would you ever go back?

You wouldn't!

In this digital world, businesses are too focused on trans-actions and hacks and funnels, and not focused enough on the people and the relationships.

Gratitude is essential to good business. When you share yourself openly, including giving thanks, you are making a connection with people. You are reaching out to them and making them feel special and cared for. This helps your business stand out.

The book you hold in your hands will show you how to use gratitude in your professional life.

To grow your business.

To build relationships.

To boost your referrals.

To have a happier workplace.

To ultimately make more money.

And, who knows, maybe with the extra money you make incorporating gratitude in your business, you'll take a life-changing trip too!

Why gratitude?

Expressing gratitude to someone doesn't just make them feel good. Turns out, thanking others boosts your happiness and decreases stress. According to Robert Emmons, PhD, author of *Thanks!: How the New Science of Gratitude Can Make You Happier*, grateful people report higher levels of positive emotions, life satisfaction, and optimism—and lower levels of depression and stress.

That's a change we could all benefit from!

In this book, I'll show you 40 ways you can use gratitude to delight your clients and build relationships with them.

I'll also show you several case studies of businesses already doing this and doing it well. In every case, their customers spend more money and refer more business. You'll learn just how simple and rewarding it is to make gratitude central to your business model.

TIP #1

Send Thank You Cards

When was the last time you received a handwritten thank you card from a business?

It doesn't happen too often, does it?

Now, the more important question: When is the last time *you* sent a thank you card to one of your clients or customers?

If you can't remember, don't worry! It's never too late to start. And it's a great habit to start practicing to set your business apart from the hundreds or thousands of other businesses you might be competing with.

The first question you might be asking yourself is: Why should I be writing and sending professional thank you cards in the first place?

Running a business is all about relationships. Whether you're a personal trainer helping people get fit, a doctor treating a patient, or an author with thousands of readers, you're in the relationship business.

And there's no better way to build relationships than through a handwritten note.

Think about it. How many emails do you get a day? Fifty? A hundred? More? Emails tend to get lost in the sea of hundreds or thousands of other emails your customer gets each month. Many of them go unopened.

A text message is quick and simple. But does it really convey a heartfelt message you took the time and care to craft? I don't think so.

Now imagine you're walking to your mailbox. You open it up to a stack of mail. You pull everything out of the mailbox and flip through the stack.

Ad, ad, bill, ad, bill.

And then you see it: an envelope with your handwritten name and address.

It's obviously a card meant just for you.

You find yourself smiling. Your mood changes. You're happy just knowing that someone took the time to sit down and write a personal note to you.

This is how your customer will feel when they receive your card in the mail.

And guess what? Unlike those emails that go unopened and then moved to the trash, handwritten cards get opened 100% of the time.

Joe Girard Sold 13,001 Cars by Sending out Thank You Cards

Probably the most famous example of someone building their business with thank you cards is the story of Joe Girard.

He's listed in the Guinness World Records as the "World's Greatest Salesman" for selling cars. And sell cars he did!

Check out some of the impressive statistics from his 14-year career selling cars at a Chevrolet dealership right outside of Detroit, Michigan:[1]

- In total, Joe sold 13,001 cars. That's more than 6 per day.
- On his best day, he sold 18 vehicles.
- His best month was 174 vehicles sold.
- In his best year, he sold 1,425 cars.

---

1   Tom Sant, The Giants of Sales (New York: AMACOM, 2006).

- By himself, Joe Girard sold more cars than 95% of all dealers in North America.

How did Joe do it? Beyond knowing how to close the deal, Joe knew the secret to sales was *building a relationship*. Every month, year after year, Girard would send a handwritten greeting card to every customer on his list. Inside they found a simple message.

Joe knew they'd need a new car one day, and he wanted to keep himself top of mind. Girard's dedication to keeping in touch with his customers instilled in them a psychological obligation to do business with him. When they needed a new car, they went straight to Joe. And when their friends needed a new car, his customers referred them to Joe.

Mary Kay Ash's Secret to Success Led Her to a 2-Billion-Dollar Business

Mary Kay Ash, founder of Mary Kay Cosmetics, was a businesswoman who knew that relationships are central to a successful business. She was known for saying: "Customer focus is truly the key. It's the real test of service, and service is the real heart of our business."

She hit the nail on the head. As a small business owner or entrepreneur, when you offer customers a genuine relationship, they'll want to do business with you again. If you treat them like a transaction, they won't feel good. The likelihood of them coming back is diminished.

I've experienced this firsthand living in Denver. My favorite coffee shop is Fluid Coffee. Yes, they make the best café au lait with almond milk, but the real reason I come back day after day is their baristas. They're friendly. They're engaging. They know my name. They smile and talk to me. They know I run a business called Say It With Gratitude, that I love Virginia basketball, and that I've traveled to Guatemala. They give me a simple hello and ask me how I'm doing. They treat me like a human.

Imagine that!

Conversely, when I lived in another part of Denver, there was a closer coffee shop I went to probably at least a dozen times. Even though I loved the atmosphere and location, I felt no connection to it. Not once did any of the baristas ask me how I was, get to know my name, or say, "Have a good day." I started to resent going to that place. It felt like a transaction.

You want to have a relational business, not a transactional one.

When Mary Kay Ash was starting out her cosmetics

business, she set herself a simple task: she handwrote three thank you notes at the end of each day. She attributed part of her success in business to taking the time to let the people around her know they were appreciated.

As a result, Mary Kay Beauty Consultants were taught the same thing—to send lots of thank you notes. After each Mary Kay party a consultant hosts, she sends thank you notes to every participant!

Here is the company's philosophy: Thank the hostess before the party and after the party. Thank the guests who purchased products, and thank the guests who didn't purchase anything but tried the products! Thank those who listened to the Mary Kay Opportunity. Thank your guests for coming to the success meetings. Thank people you do business with. Thank sister consultants. And thank directors.

What you give out comes back to you tenfold.

The following best practices are a few examples of how consultants make their customers feel extra special after buying a product. You can easily adapt some of these to your industry.

- It's important for your customers to receive their product as soon as you can deliver it. Having product on hand makes a really big difference, and it's an investment that will definitely boost your sales. Not only will your customers know they can count on you when they run out of something and need it "now," they will be more likely to refer you to their friends.

- Add a postcard with maybe your family picture to the order as a thank you with a few fun things you offer to your clients, like the Preferred Customer Program, etc. ...

- If you are delivering to your customer at her office, tie an inexpensive pink helium balloon to their bag when making the delivery. Others in the office will see the service your customers are getting.

- If you are sending anything through the mail, make the products look important. Wrap everything in tissue or elegant printed paper. Using white sparkly tissue paper is a nice touch. Spray a little bit of any fragrance inside the box so when your customer opens it, it smells great!

- Always write "Thank You!" and then sign your name in your handwriting with a smiley face on every invoice.

- In their order, place some chocolate! They will LOVE this! Think about purchasing the DOVE

Chocolates because they have inspirational sayings and quotes inside of the wrapper.

- Always write a thank you "snail mail" card that may say something like this after a party:

Hi _____!

May this find you having an incredible and richly blessed day! It was so nice to meet you at _____'s Mary Kay party! Thank you for the opportunity to pamper you! I had so much fun! (or it was such a treat!)

Thank you for your Mary Kay purchase too! I hope you are having fun with your new beauty goodies and always know that everything, even if you have used it, is 100% guaranteed! I will call you in a few days to follow up and answer any questions you may have. Thank you for the opportunity to be your Mary Kay Beauty Consultant and thank you for your business.

Sincerely, (Your name)

You may want to send a "Thank you Letter" explaining the benefits of being your customer and the fun things you do throughout the year! For example: Mary Kay Money (for every $10 they spend throughout the year, they earn a $1 to spend at your annual open house!), Birthday Month Discount, etc.[2]

To date, Mary Kay Cosmetics has grown to a 2-billion-dollar industry, and a big reason is because of the way they treat their customers like people instead of a transaction.

Millions More in Donations for Non-Profits

Sending thank you cards benefits non-profits as well.

DonorsChoose.org is probably the best-known example of how handwritten thank you notes can help a non-profit receive more donations. Julia Prieto tells the story of how the organization got its start:

> *In 2000, almost a decade before "crowdfunding" became a buzzword, Charles Best, a high school teacher at Wings Academy in the Bronx, created a platform to fund classroom projects for teachers. After a slow start, teachers across the Bronx soon heard about the site, posting hundreds of projects.*
>
> *The story that often doesn't make the cut is what*

---

2   Adapted from "Customer Service Tips: Build Customers for Life," accessed August 14, 2018, http://debbieelbrecht.com/uploads/3/4/6/9/34697515/customer_service_tips.pdf.

happened next, how his students helped those early projects get funded.

The high schoolers at Wings Academy, after seeing firsthand what the site was capable of, took matters into their own hands. They volunteered every day after school to hand-address letters to potential donors across the country. They mailed 2,000 letters. And those 2,000 letters resulted in $30,000—in other words, the first major wave of real DonorsChoose.org donations.[3]

Since then, the entire business model of DonorsChoose. org has integrated handwritten thank you notes. After a project has been successfully funded, students create handwritten thank you packages that they send to the donors who funded their projects. In one year they sent over 75,000 envelopes to donors filled with a half a million notes from students.

Of course, the good folks over at DonorsChoose.org wanted to see if the handwritten notes were making a difference in the amount of donations they received. In an experiment to measure the ROI of their non-profit, the staff of Donors Choose sent handwritten thank you notes to half of all recent first-time donors.

---

3   Julia Prieto, "How We Leverage Gratitude to Drive a Business Model," The DonorsChoose Blog, Nov. 24, 2015, https://www. donorschoose.org/blog/power-of-student-thank you-notes/.

The results? They found that 38% of people who received a thank you note were more likely to give again than those who didn't receive one. Recipients of the thank you notes donate an additional $41 per year on average, translating to more than $3 million in additional donations per year!

Practical Steps to Writing Thank You Cards

You might be wondering if there's a process for writing thank you cards. Great news! There actually is. I sat down with Steven Littlefield, author of *The Business of Gratitude*, for an interview as part of my Grateful Entrepreneur Summit, and he outlined his 5-step process for writing thank you cards:

1. **Forge a gratitude mindset.** First, understand that what you focus on expands. The gratitude mind-set starts with being present and focusing on what is available to you today to be grateful for. If you're reading this, you're still breathing. You have your eyesight. Start with being grateful for the things you might take for granted. So the gratitude mind-set is focusing on everything that you can be grateful for.

   Then start focusing on people to be thankful for. Think about the people who are important in your life. When is the last time you expressed gratitude for them with a thank you note? Make a list of people to write and mail cards to.

And so that's the gratitude mind-set: focus on *who* you can thank today.

2. **Get organized.** Getting organized to send out thank you cards involves 4 things: You need an envelope, a thank you card, a pen, and a stamp to mail the card.

   Stephen suggests an optional 5th item—your business card. I don't recommend putting your business card in a thank you card. If you're sending thank you cards, it's about thanking those people and showing them that you care. You're deepening the relationship and building trust, not soliciting a transaction. This is a way to say thank you in an honorable way and be truly appreciative.

3. **Write to connect.** Have you ever been at an event where you meet somebody and you hit it off? Sometimes you just meet people that you instantly get along with, and you say, "We've got to stay in touch." But then time gets away from you and you never get in touch again. That's happened to all of us!

   Start to develop this habit of writing to connect.

When you meet somebody for the first time and you're at an event and they've met 45 other people, how do you remind them who you are and where you met them? You follow up with them by sending a handwritten card in the mail. And make a connection.

Here's an example: "Dear Scott, Thank you. It was a pleasure meeting you at the Rockies game. I really appreciate it. [Write one thing you talked about, such as: I appreciated you sharing your ideas on fitness with me]. I would really like to follow up and continue that conversation. Feel free to give me a call or email me a good time to connect."

So it's a very simple way to remind them of how you met and of the conversation you had. In a non-threatening way, it opens the door for them to get back to you.

4. **Sending cards for all occasions.** There are so many occasions to send someone a card in the mail. You can always thank somebody when you've first met them. You can thank someone for doing a good job. You can thank someone for getting on the phone with you to talk about business.

You can also send a card just to congratulate somebody on a special event, an anniversary, or a promotion. You can send a card for sympathy if somebody loses a loved one, or a "get well" note if they're in the hospital recovering from an injury or surgery.

The business of gratitude is being grateful for people in a caring way. Connect with someone when they're going through a difficult time. You can say: "I understand you're going through a tough time. I just want you to know that you're in my thoughts, my heart, my prayers. If you need someone to reach out to, I'm here for you."

One of the most powerful notes Stephen writes is the "regret." He shares an example from his industry. In the mortgage business, not everybody's approved for their loan. Even when you approve someone for a loan, they sometimes get their loans somewhere else. So Stephen will send a note, even on that occasion: "Thank you for giving me the opportunity to work with you. I regret that I wasn't able to serve your needs at this time. In today's business world, things change. So if anything changes in your world, feel free to contact me."

Writing this note keeps the door open. Stephen says it got him more business because people would send him referrals, or they'd come back to him when their credit got fixed or their job became more stable.

5. **Magnetize referrals.** One of the best ways to keep people's mind on you is to thank them for a referral—even if the referral ends up not buying your product or service. That's how you magnetize business. You immediately reward the referring person no matter what happens. This is called "random reinforcement."

   When you reinforce people's behavior, they will continue that behavior. Every time someone sends you the name and phone number of a potential customer, you should send them a thank you note to reinforce that behavior. The note can say something like: "Thank you for your kind referral of Scott Colby. I look forward to taking great care of his financing options, and I will follow up with you as we progress."

   Now they know that you got the referral, they feel good that they gave you a referral, and they want that feeling again. They're going to want to send you more referrals, and your business will multiply.

As part of The Grateful Entrepreneur online summit, I interviewed several other people who are using thank you cards to grow their business. They're cultivating relationships with customers, increasing retention, and getting more referrals. I highlight a few of them below.

You can download all of the interviews at www.sayitwithgratitude.com/bonuses.

Increase Retention By 50%

Nae Morris is the head of the support team at Wufoo, a software company that allows you to build online forms. Wufoo is known for sending thank you cards to customers every week. The team takes time to draft, decorate, and mail personalized cards to their customers, a tradition that dates back to their early days.

And get this—out of the roughly 800 customers who received handwritten cards last year, 50% fewer customers left Wufoo than those who did not receive cards.

So think about that: in Wufoo's experience, retention rates are 50% better among customers who received a thank you note!

I'm left wondering, if thank you cards make such good business sense, why aren't all companies sending them?

I love Wufoo's approach: They write their cards as a team every Thursday. This allows the team to bond through sharing the task, joking, and building relationships with each other. The card writing also allows them to feel closer with their customers.

Nae said as a manager, she loves being able to see her team building those bonds, working together, laughing, and talking about their weekend plans. She's seen how this project allows them to deepen their relationships. They are getting to know each other on a personal level. She's seen that trust has grown among team members as a result. This has been an invaluable way of increasing employees' happiness. And it's all because they're working to make their customers happy with thank you cards!

Be Vulnerable with Your Customers

I love the way Yasmin Nguyen thinks about writing thank you cards. Yasmin is the founder of The Joyful Living Project, and I had the opportunity to sit down and talk to him about gratitude. First of all, he calls thank you cards "appreciation cards," which I love! He likes to create a deeper connection through his cards, allowing himself to be vulnerable.

Yasmin starts his cards by writing something like: "Dear Scott. I remember the time when ..."

The purpose of starting the cards like this is to reconnect to a memorable moment. It should call to mind something special in the recipient.

He continues by saying something like, "What I appreciate most about you is ..." So it's not necessarily something the person did; it's about a quality they possess, something about them that Yasmin appreciates.

The final part of the card is where Yasmin thinks to himself, *If today were my last day, what would I want this person to know?* This allows him to go really deep in terms of what he wants to share with the recipient.

This process creates an element of vulnerability. It's an approach designed to help you put yourself in a happy place and fuel your writing. Writing and sending heartfelt cards like this has opened so many doors for Yasmin. He's witnessed new connections and growth in his business.

Think about it: How often do you receive a card from someone simply to reconnect with you and tell you of an attribute they cherish in you? What would you be willing to do for that?

Treat Your Customers Like Family

Doug Spurling is the owner of Spurling Fitness, a gym in Kennebunk, Maine. I could tell when I interviewed Doug that customer experience is one of the top values for his company. What impressed me even more is that he's built a system of sending out handwritten cards on a regular basis—not just when a new member joins his gym.

Here's his process:

- When a new client signs up to his gym, not only will his admin write a thank you card, but the whole team will sign it. So the client instantly feels welcomed to the family.

- The 6-week mark is a common time for new clients to lose their motivation and stop coming to the gym. So the client's trainer will write a hand-written letter appreciating him or her for being a part of the family and highlight 1–2 wins they've accomplished in the first 6 weeks.

- They also send out a handwritten note at the 6-month mark and again at the 1-year mark to celebrate and appreciate the client.

You can even use cards to reactivate old clients. Doug

does this well. He sends out "we miss you" letters, which get mailed to clients approximately 6 months after they leave the gym.

Why would you do this? Well, if you don't send out a letter like this, the client may never think about you. It's the old top-of-mind awareness idea. Remember Joe Girard, the car salesman, talking about that?

Doug and his team send a letter to old clients saying something like, "Hey, Sally! I hope life is great. We miss having you as part of the family." And then Doug always gives them a little incentive to come back, perhaps a small discount, and the whole team signs the card.

Close New Business with Cards

Curtis Lewsey is a real estate agent in Florida who has mastered the art of appreciation. It seems fitting then that he's one of the co-authors of the book *Appreciation Marketing*.

When I interviewed Curtis, he shared a nugget of advice. If you're following up with a prospect and wanting to close the deal, send them a card with this sentence in it: "I appreciate the opportunity to earn your business." Just by using this one strategy, Curtis has helped clients land business! He's seen this approach work successfully for all kinds of businesspeople—from executives closing private jet deals to landscapers getting new landscaping customers.

Curtis also recommends that when you're talking to a prospect on the phone, you always ask when the best time you can follow up with them would be. And then have a system in place to consistently follow up!

TIP #2

Build Authentic Relationships to Generate Referrals

If there's an authority on how to grow a business by building relationships and getting more referrals using greeting cards, it's my mentor David Frey. David's greeting card sales team has sold over $4 million dollars' worth of greeting cards. He's the author of the Instant Referral Systems program and the *Small Business Marketing Bible*. He used to conduct referral marketing seminars all over the United States.

David's #1 tip for business owners is to create more touch points with their customers. He paints a clear picture with this example:

> *Let's say there are two couples. Couple #1 doesn't talk at all for 30 days. No conversation at all. Couple #2 talks every single day and has positive conversations.*

At the end of the 30 days, who do you think will have the better relationship? It's obvious, right? Couple #2!

Relationships are built on constant communication and positive experiences. Stephen Covey explores the idea of your emotional bank account in his book *The Seven Habits of Highly Effective People*. Everybody has an emotional bank account; and that emotional bank account is different for every relationship in your life. Your goal is to make continual deposits into people's emotional bank account to make them feel good about you. The way you do that is through different communication touch points.

With the advent of new technology, we have the opportunity to create many more touch points with our clients and patients than ever before in the history of humankind. We've got text messaging, social media (Facebook, Instagram, Snapchat, and Twitter), email, direct mail, phone calls, webinars, videos, and even messaging that goes straight to voicemail.

I had the opportunity to sit down with David as part of The Grateful Entrepreneur Summit. David said that if he were looking for the most effective relationship-building system that leads to more referrals, he would look for a system that had the following criteria:

- Something that can be personalized so the client knows you took time to think about them.

- Something that has the potential to pull their heartstrings. People want to have meaningful relationships with other people, not just "Facebook friend" relationships.

- Something that shows you took time to reach out to them. A greeting card requires you to pick a card, write a message, and send it in the mail. It's not like an email where you just write it and click a button. Emails don't cut it.

- Something that can leverage your time, meaning something that can touch many people in a short amount of time.

- Something that is low cost with a high emotional ROI. If you're going to touch a lot of people, it needs to be within your budget. If you're a solo business owner or a very small company, you probably don't have the budget to take 100 of your clients to a pro basketball game.

- Something that also adds value to their lives. Something that might teach them things they didn't know or a tool they can use. Something that builds your reputation and creates trust.

- Something that you can touch and feel. People are

getting so many messages using technology that they are craving something that exists in the real world.

- Something that lingers. It needs to be something that lingers for a while so the positive effects of the deposit into their emotional bank account will last.

- And something that doesn't take a lot of work. Most professionals are very busy people. They don't have a large staff. They don't have the time or expertise to run large-scale, complex relationship-building tasks.

Can you guess the #1 relationship-building and relationship-maintaining tool David has used? That's right—the handwritten greeting card!

You can write a heartfelt email. That email may never get opened if it winds up in the spam folder. And not everybody checks email these days because they get so many. Sometimes we're just sick of email. The handwritten note is such an underutilized tool, but it's something that everyone can start using today. You can send out one card and touch somebody's life in a deep emotional way.

Why do handwritten greeting cards work so well as a relationship builder? Because they meet all of the criteria David mentioned above!

- You can personalize a greeting card.

- You can write personal, heartfelt, authentic messages that tug on people's heartstrings.

- A card shows you took the time out of your life to do something nice for the recipient.

- You can leverage your time by sending out hundreds of greeting cards in a short period of time. Especially if you use a system or service.

- Greeting cards are low cost. They might cost a few bucks to send. That's cheap. It brings a very high ROI to your marketing dollar. Most small business owners can afford to do that.

- Also, along with putting personal, heartfelt messages in the card, you can include tips and tactics on the other side of the card to add value to their lives.

- People love greeting cards because you can touch and feel them with your hands. They're not emails, which can get lost in the shuffle. They're not voicemails. They're not text messages. They're not private Facebook messages. They're something you hold in your hands.

- Greeting cards linger. They aren't quickly thrown away like other business mail. People will keep their greeting cards around for a long time. You even see greeting cards displayed on refrigerators for months!

- And if you use a system or a service to help you write and send your cards, they can be done really fast.

Sending handwritten cards is about the best thing you can do to build relationships with customers, short of meeting with your clients face to face.

An Easy System to Get More Referrals with Handwritten Cards

Here are five "rules" David suggests following when sending greeting cards to clients:

1. Never mix a thank you card or a "just checking in" card or a relationship-building card with a referral message. That turns people off. Never put your business card in your thank you cards. If you're going to send out a heartfelt greeting card, then make it a heartfelt greeting card. If you're going to send out a card asking for a referral, then make that card about the referral and nothing else. Keep your heartfelt messages and your business messages on separate cards.

2. Use the 3:1 ratio. As mentioned earlier, everyone

has an emotional bank account. After years of sending cards, David found a 3:1 ratio works well. Initiate three deposits into a personal emotional bank account before making a withdrawal. Asking for a referral is a withdrawal from a person's emotional bank account. So send out a heartfelt card for three months to the same person to build the relationship; on the fourth month, send out a card asking for a referral.

3. Frequency is key to staying top of mind. Email marketers will tell you that emailing daily is the best frequency balance for the highest ROI. David suggests sending a greeting card to a client on a monthly basis, so people always remember you. They'll also know that you're serious about your relationship with them.

4. Add value in your cards. If you're going to send cards monthly, make sure you are adding some type of value beyond the heartfelt message in the card. Add some tips or even a funny illustration— something that will make them want to open your card every month.

5. Every fourth month, send a referral request card. So if you're following David's 3:1 rule, you should

be asking your client for referrals three times a year.

Now imagine if you were sending your cards to 200 clients. That would amount to asking your clients for referrals 600 times a year. If you're asking your clients 600 times a year, your referrals are going to take off like never before because the vast majority of business owners aren't currently asking for referrals at all! Imagine going from asking for referrals 0 times to 600 times, but in a very authentic way.

Remember, you're sending three relationship-building cards before you ever send that referral request card. They're going to be okay with that referral request card because you're sending three times the amount of value to them, right? Three deposits in the emotional bank account, one withdrawal; everything is cool. It works! David's seen it with his own eyes.

Over the years, David has worked with a number of different service-based professionals to help them get more referrals with greeting cards. Anyone from real estate agents to insurance agents, from mortgage brokers to dentists. His system works!

When the time came for David to move on to other projects, he passed the baton to us at Say It With

Gratitude. We've adapted David's model of helping businesses get more referrals with cards, and it's a service we now offer to businesses. If you see this model working well for your business, you can learn more at sayitwithgratitude.com/pages/grow-your-business.

I asked David if he could provide some examples of what to say when asking for a referral. He provided a few referral card templates, so you'll know exactly what to write. You can download them at www.sayitwithgratitude.com/bonuses.

When you download the referral card templates, notice that David's not saying, "Will you please send me referrals?" We're simply reaffirming that they enjoyed the service we provided. We're reaffirming that they got value out of that service and they have a friend who's having the same problem. Will you mention me to your friend? That's all we're asking, right? Isn't that beautiful?

This is Relationship Marketing 101. There is no hard selling. All you want to do is remind your customer that you're out there. Remind them about what you do. Most importantly, remind them that referrals are important to your business. And that's how you grow your business with referrals and handwritten cards.

TIP #3

Send out Cards on Weird Holidays to Stand Out from the Crowd

A lot of businesses send out holiday cards at Christmas. You can stand apart and do something different by sending cards on more unique holidays, such as Groundhog Day, St. Patrick's Day, or the Fourth of July! Thanksgiving is a good one too, since it's a holiday specifically to express gratitude.

Here's a good example of how sending out handwritten notes on different holidays can help your business: Jon Bockman owns Bockman's Auto Care in Sycamore, Illinois. For the past 8 years, he has spent an average of $1,858 per year on thank you cards for his entire customer base.

That might seem like a lot, right? Well, Jon has consistently seen between a $35,000 and $45,000 return on his yearly Thanksgiving and "Christmas in July" cards, which tell each customer in his database simply, "Thank you."

Bockman doesn't send out weekly thank you cards. Instead, he sends them out semiannually. And when his Christmas cards weren't showing an ROI, he realized it was because so many businesses send out Christmas thank you cards. So he started sending out thank you notes on less-recognized holidays.[4]

You can find a list of all kinds of weird holidays here at holidayinsights.com/moreholidays/.

---

4   Travis Bean, "A Thank You Card that Stands out from the Crowd," Ratchet + Wrench, Dec. 7, 2017, https://www.ratchetandwrench.com/articles/5348-a-thank-you-card-that-stands-out-from-the-crowd.

TIP #4
Offer Sympathy

How many businesses send out sympathy cards when a family member of a customer or employee passes away? Practically none. Your business should do so. Send a heartfelt handwritten sympathy card when your customers lose loved ones.

It's never easy to write a note of condolence because the subject is death. It's hard to know what to say. The challenge is to strike just the right tone and choose your words carefully. The wrong words can make a poor impression and even damage the business/professional relationship.

Realize that writing a condolence note is not about being profound. It's about acknowledging a death and expressing genuine sympathy. That's it! I like the wording suggested by Florence Isaacs:

> *Dear Janet,*
>
> *I'm so sorry to hear about your mother's passing. You are in my thoughts and prayers at this time of sadness. I send my deepest condolences.*

Follow with your signature. Here is another option:

> *Dear Janet,*
>
> *I just heard about your mother's death. I'm so sorry for your loss. Please accept my heartfelt sympathy.*

And simply sign your name. Such brief notes are both powerful and appropriate.[5]

Do your best to avoid these common mistakes in writing words of condolence:

- Being overly dramatic: "I am absolutely heartbroken for you."

- Being cliché: "Time will heal all wounds."

- Being too impersonal and formal: "Our sincere condolences to you on behalf of your unfortunate loss."

---

5   Florence Isaacs, "How to Write a Condolence Note to a Customer or Client," Legacy connect, May 17, 2013, http://connect.legacy.com/profiles/blogs/how-to-write-a-condolence-note-to-a-customer-or-client.

- Offering advice: "When the days seem dark, remember to cherish the good memories the two of you created. It will help carry you through the dark."[6]

I personally also send sympathy cards when a customer loses a pet. Our furry friends are family too, and clients will truly appreciate the gesture.

---

6   Jenna Marie, "What to Write in Business Sympathy Cards," Simple Sympathy, Aug. 11, 2013, http://simplesympathy.com/business-sympathy-cards.html.

TIP #5

Have Customer Appreciation Parties

If you have a brick-and-mortar business, throw a customer appreciation party. You could team up with another local business. Let's say you own a gym. Partner with a hair salon or fitness apparel store. They can host the party and provide food and wine—and they can provide a discount to your clients.

I used to run a bootcamp business specifically for women from 2005–2010 when I lived in Dallas. It was called Her Strength, and we had a couple of appreciation parties for the bootcamp members. The first time we threw a customer appreciation party, we partnered with Lucy apparel store. They hosted the party and provided wine and light snacks. My bootcamp members got free wine and snacks and discounts on apparel that evening. Lucy got new customers. And I was providing goodwill to my members. Goodwill to your clients will make them want to stick around longer and continue using your services.

We had another customer appreciation party at a local makeup store in Dallas. They hosted it, provided free wine and cheese, and pampered my bootcamp members by doing their makeup. The store also gave my members discounts that evening with any purchase. And purchase they did! The makeup store got a lot of new customers out of that event.

A client appreciation party is one of the ultimate ways to show your gratitude. Your clients are happy because they feel appreciated, and—if you set it up right—they get free food and drinks, and a good deal on products. The partnering business is happy because they are getting new customers and making sales. You're happy because you're showing gratitude in the form of goodwill to your clients—and you know they'll be loyal to you as a result.

It's a win-win-win!

TIP #6

Give Personalized Gifts

It's fun to send unexpected gifts to others. It doesn't have to be something big, flashy, or expensive. It's the thought that counts. It's the element of surprise that makes it so much fun.

The key is to make your gift personalized and meaningful to the recipient. I see a lot of fitness professionals asking for advice about what kinds of gifts to get their clients during the holidays. The answer is always a yoga mat, a set of resistance bands, a Starbucks gift card, or something along those lines. These clients have spent hundreds or thousands of dollars on your business, and you're just going to get them a generic gift?

Bad idea!

A personalized gift goes so much further by providing meaning for your customer. Even better, make it a gift their spouse or the whole family can enjoy!

Recently, I sat down to talk about this topic with John Ruhlin, author of *Giftology*. His firm specializes in teaching fast-growing service firms how to stand out, be memorable, and become even more referable through gift-giving.

John reinforced this idea of giving a personalized gift. In fact, he often gives really nice Cutco knives as gifts to his best customers. He even has the gift engraved with the customer's name on it.

When John was just starting out in business, he got some advice from a successful businessman: "John, in 40 years in business, the reason I have more referrals and deal flow than I could ever imagine is I found that if you take care of the family and invest in them, everything else seems to take care of itself in business."

I asked John what business owners should *NOT* do when it comes to giving gifts to customers. He said you shouldn't only target the executive or decision-maker. Most of the time, the admin or the secretary is the forgotten employee. Make them feel appreciated too.

John's not a big fan of giving consumables as gifts. What if your customer is on a diet, and you send her some chocolates? What if your customer's wife is gluten free, and you send the family something that contains wheat?

What if you send a customer a bottle of wine, but she's a recovering alcoholic? None of these gifts would make a good impression.

When giving gifts, think about cost per impression. If you spend $50 on a gift basket, you get 1 impression. The customer eats the contents, and the gift is gone. And it cost you $50. On the other hand, imagine that you spend $500 on a knife set or a custom leather folio. It's more money up front, but 10 years later, it might have gotten 3,000 impressions (3,000 uses). And your gift basket only got 1. So your cost of impression for the more expensive gift is actually a better value.

Another tip when it comes to gift giving is: Don't put your logo on it. Don't make your gift a promotion for your business. That's about you—not your recipient.

Can you imagine going into a wedding and having your name engraved on the wedding gift that you give to the happy couple? Even the cheesiest marketer on the planet wouldn't show up at a wedding carrying a Tiffany's vase with their own logo engraved on the side. If somebody's getting married, you engrave their name, their spouse's name, and their wedding date. You make the gift all about them. But for some reason, in business we try to combine a promotional marketing tool with a gift. That's not a gift. It's a promotional tool. And it's self-serving. It's not a heartfelt expression of appreciation.

Even when you give somebody an expensive set of Bose headphones and you put your logo on the side, you're trying to turn them into a billboard. Your customer doesn't receive this as a gift. Instead, they feel manipulated, like you're getting them to promote your brand. Oftentimes, they'll give your gift to someone else. Or they won't use it. They might even scratch off the logo you actually paid money to put on there!

If you're going to give a gift, make it all about your customer. Put their name on it, put their logo on it. Think about it: If I gave you a Rolex, would I have to put my name on it in order for you to remember where it came from? No.

Don't make the gift about you. Make it about them. In doing so, they will shine the spotlight back on you when the time is appropriate, by referring customers to you and opening doors for you.

When it comes to gift-giving, here's one of John's best tips: Give gifts that are best in class.

If you're giving a $100 watch to people who have Rolexes and other nice watches, they'll never wear it. However,

If you give a $50 mug that's absolutely the best in its class, the customer will use it and think of you. They'll probably show it off to friends too!

I interviewed Alicia Streger, a business coach for fitness professionals, and I love her gifting philosophy. Her focus is surprise and delight. Every single week she and her team pick three to five random clients to send a gift to and make their day special. So now it's not just sending cards and gifts as a thank you because clients gave you money and bought your program. It's about surprising your customers with delight. The element of surprise goes a long way. Treat people like family. Think about a person whose day you can make great. And then do it! As a bonus, people will often take pictures of the gift and post it on social media, giving you and your business some exposure.

Here's a great example: my friend and business coach, Pat Rigsby, loves Disney. I mean loves it! He loves the company, he loves the experience they provide, and he loves taking his family to Disney World—several times a year.

During the Christmas holiday of 2017, I got clued in that he was going to be there for a few days, checking into the Wilderness Lodge at Disney late on December

26. If you're wondering how I figured this out, I asked Pat's right-hand man, Matt. I know, sneaky, huh?

Wanting to do something nice for Pat because of his help as my business coach, I decided to order Pat and his family a Disney tote bag with a bunch of treats in it. I scheduled it to be at their hotel the day they arrived.

It worked like a charm! They were completely surprised, and I'm guessing the kids were really happy to see the bag of treats that showed up in their hotel room. The only thing that didn't get executed properly? My name was left off the card as the sender of the gift. So Pat had no idea who it was from for a few days until Matt told him. Oops.

TIP # 7

Give Away Something Because Your Customers Are Awesome!

Show your appreciation to your customers by doing a giveaway from time to time. I think it's more meaningful to do this on an individual basis, as it shows you truly care about your customers as people. It makes a statement that you aren't in it purely for the profit. I've done this on numerous occasions and would like to share a couple of my most recent examples, both from my fitness business.

I recently launched some new fitness and nutrition programs. I learned that one of my Fit For Photos clients was interested in them, but she'd had some medical challenges for the past year or so. She'd been suffering from Lyme disease and basically felt like she had a chronic case of the flu. The past year had been the most debilitating of her life, and it sounded awful. She said she believed a paleo autoimmune eating plan would help alleviate some of her symptoms. Well, I happen to have a paleo autoimmune meal plan that I sell for $49.

This client has been a customer of mine for years, and now I learn that she's really suffering. I have something that can help her. Why try and milk $49 out of her when I can be kind and give her the plan at no cost as a way of saying thank you for being an awesome person? So that's what I did.

Another long-time Fit For Photos client of mine was going through some personal challenges, but in a different way. Without going into the messy details, I can tell you she'll be raising her three kids alone on a social worker's salary, but she wants to continue doing my fitness programs to help her navigate this rough patch she's going through. The workouts help her stress level and keep her strong—both inside and out. She's been a client of mine for a long time, and she's always been supportive of the other people going through my programs.

I could charge her $59 for the program, like I do every other customer. But instead of milking every dollar out of her at a time when her personal life is rocky, why not give her the program as my way of saying thanks?

I realize that you're running a business and not a charity.

But when you take an opportunity to reward your best customers, you will have them for life!

TIP #8
Provide a Free Bonus

Not everything has to be an upsell. And you don't have to milk every dollar from your client. Show your appreciation by giving them a free bonus from time to time.

Or surprise them with a free upgrade. The element of surprise is a powerful thing, and if you thank your customers with a free, spontaneous upgrade, they will love you for a long time. You could pick five customers at random and give them an upgrade, or even choose your most loyal customers and surprise them.

Airlines mastered this years ago with their frequent flyer programs, which promotes brand loyalty, and they often upgrade passengers to business or first class. The industry isn't doing so hot these days, though. Come to think of it, I should probably send each airline a copy of this book!

I've seen fitness companies sell their workout programs

online and then try to upsell clients on the diet. C'mon! Don't do that. A nutrition and workout program go hand in hand. Clients need both to get results, so the programs should be sold together as a fitness package instead of separately. That's what I mean when I say you don't have to milk every dollar from your client. They won't like it.

I'll give you an example of how my company, Say It With Gratitude, takes a different approach. This year, we're putting on an experience called the Gratitude Trek, which is a 4-day camping and hiking adventure in the Sierra Mountains. It's a full-service, high-end mountain experience, and I want to make sure my clients receive special treatment.

The clients who are going on the Gratitude Trek should have a certain level of fitness. So for everyone who signs up for the Gratitude Trek, I'm gifting them a 9-week fitness coaching program to get them in shape for the 4-day outing! Just my little way of saying thank you. Instead of upselling them on this 9-week fitness program and trying to make a few extra bucks, I'd rather show them my appreciation.

Banks are notorious for giving bonuses to help close new business, offering up to $400 when you open an account with them. I remember back when I was a kid my parents got a free microwave when opening a bank account. This was back when microwaves were fairly new. This is a gratitude technique that never goes out of style!

TIP #9

Offer Free Goodies

If you have an actual store location, provide coffee, food, or some other small gift or treat for customers who come into the store.

Trader Joe's, a grocery store chain, always has complimentary coffee at the front of the store. This freebie lets the store showcase different types of coffee they carry; meanwhile, shoppers get the chance to try before they buy and have a warming cup of joe while browsing the aisles.

I've gone to high-end clothing boutiques that offer a free glass of wine or a martini while you shop and try on clothes. Hey, maybe having a little alcohol in you will get you to buy more. And it's fun!

In Denver, there's a cookie company called Marsha's Cookies that always has a table at my favorite farmers market in the summer. She must have about 20 different kinds of cookies, and she provides samples of each flavor. Wouldn't you know it, every time I sample one of her cookies, I always leave buying three of them! Too bad it's not great for my waistline.

People love free, people love food—thus, people love free food. Retailers, too, have their own reasons to love sampling, from the financial (samples have boosted sales in some cases by as much as 2,000%)[7] to the behavioral (they can sway people to habitually buy things that they never purchased previously).

In an article for *The Atlantic*, Joe Pinsker writes:

> *There's no brand that's as strongly associated with free samples as Costco. Costco knows that sampling, if done right, can convince people that its stores are fun places to be.*

> *"When we compare it to other in-store mediums ... in-store product demonstration has the highest [sales] lift," says Giovanni DeMeo of the product-demonstration company Interactions, a department of which handles Costco's samples. That department is Club*

---

7   Elliot Zwiebach, "Marsh increases in-store sampling," Supermarket News, Feb. 28, 2005, https://www.supermarketnews.com/archive/marsh-increases-store-sampling.

Demonstration Services, and it—not Costco—staffs the sample tables.[8]

I remember going into a Costco store and watching a demonstration of the Blendtec blender. The guy providing the demonstration made a delicious "ice cream" with spinach in it. Now THAT is a way to get me to eat my green veggies that my mom never thought of.

Anyway, I didn't buy a Blendtec there, but later on I did buy a refurbished one from the Blendtec website. But that spinach ice cream demonstration left enough of an impression on me that I'm writing about it in this book, several years later.

Pinsker's article goes on to say:

> *While DeMeo insists that the short-term spike in sales isn't the only effect of product sampling that matters—it's great for making customers loyal to stores and brands over longer periods of time—the figures are impressive. In the past year, Interactions' beer samples at many national retailers on average boosted sales by*

---

8   Joe Pinsker, "The Psychology Behind Costco's Free Samples," The Atlantic, Oct. 1, 2014, https://www.theatlantic.com/business/archive/2014/10/the-psychology-behind-costcos-free-samples/380969/.

71 percent, and its samples of frozen pizza increased sales by 600 percent.

It's true that free samples help consumers learn more about products and that they make retail environments more appealing. But samples are operating on a more subconscious level as well. "Reciprocity is a very, very strong instinct," says Dan Ariely, a behavioral economist at Duke University. "If somebody does something for you"—such as giving you a quarter of a ravioli on a piece of wax paper—"you really feel a rather surprisingly strong obligation to do something back for them."

Ariely adds that free samples can make forgotten cravings become more salient. "What samples do is they give you a particular desire for something," he says. "If I gave you a tiny bit of chocolate, all of a sudden it would remind you about the exact taste of chocolate and would increase your craving."[9]

Online businesses can do this as well. I know Amazon allows you to download free samples of books, which essentially amounts to the first few pages. There have been countless times I've finished reading the free

---

9   Pinsker, "The Psychology Behind Costco's Free Samples."

sample of the book and immediately bought the book in order to keep reading.

So think about "free samples" you can give away in your business, whether it's online or in store. Just make sure you choose carefully what you distribute so it's good for your customers and good for your business.

TIP #10
Give Away Your Service for Free

Stephanie Jones, author of *The Giving Challenge*, was another one of my interview guests for The Grateful Entrepreneur Summit. During our interview, she talked about a time when she received a free taxi ride. Here's the story in her own words:

> *I was on a business trip, taking a taxi to the airport, and my driver, Don, and I just got to talking. You know, I'm big on building connections with people who are around you, especially when you're traveling.*
>
> *The funny thing is while we were talking, he said, "Hey, you should write a book."*
>
> *And I was like, "Oh, I actually am. It's on giving."*
>
> *Well, through our conversation I found out he only took cash. But much to my dismay, I had no cash on me! So I broke Rule #1 when you travel: You should always have cash. I didn't have any, and I began to*

panic internally and said a little prayer trying to figure out what I was going to do. When we arrived at the airport, Don said, "You know what? I'm just gonna give your ride for free today. You know, a gift from me."

And I was so taken back by that because he didn't have to do it. When you're a taxi driver and you're driving one person, you're losing out on other business. So that just really touched my heart. And I felt like I needed to write about it. It perfectly illustrates a great example of a gift that you can give in your business. I often laugh about it because I said, "You know, he gave it to me expecting nothing." That was my definition of giving on my giving journey: Give something and expect nothing in return. Well, I've put him in my book. Whenever friends travel to DC, I say they should call him. And now we're talking about him here today on this interview.

I'll take it one step further: now we're talking about him in *The Grateful Entrepreneur* book too!

You can download Stephanie's full interview at www.sayitwithgratitude.com/bonuses.

TIP #11
Give Away Books

There are so many great business and personal development books out there. Give one as a gift to customers. There's nothing like receiving a book in the mail, especially when it's a surprise.

This shows that you're interested in the well-being and personal growth of your customers. One of my favorite books to give away is *The Miracle Morning,* by Hal Elrod, which teaches you how to set up a morning routine for success. *The Miracle Morning* is something everyone can benefit from, which is why it makes such a great gift!

Of course, now that I have my own book, the one you're holding in your hands, I'll be giving away plenty of copies as gifts. Ha!

I frequently run 5-day challenges for my online fitness members, and more often than not, the winner gets a book. Sometimes I'll even give them three books to choose from!

Make sure to write a personalized note inside the book so your customer knows this is a thank you meant just for them!

TIP #12

Get Together with Your Customers on the Road

If you have customers that don't live near you, make it a point to meet them when you're traveling. If you're going to a conference or traveling for pleasure, let your customers know where you'll be. You can simply make a post on Facebook or send out an email to your newsletter list.

If anyone lives in the town you'll be in, take them out to breakfast or coffee. Nothing beats meeting your customers in person. And they will be thrilled.

A customer often feels like a number or a transaction.

How many times do we call a company and hear one voice recording after another trying to get us to the right department, so someone can answer our questions, only to be put on hold for 30 minutes? It feels like we're not important. When you call a company and someone actually answers on the first ring, you're thrilled to hear a live voice.

Imagine how thrilled your customers and clients will feel when you take the time to actually meet them in person when you happen to be in the same town. They'll get to know you, like you, and trust you that much more.

I recently did this when I was in Orlando for a Mastermind meeting. I'll often post my travel plans on Facebook. On this particular occasion, one of my online fitness clients, Sherry, was traveling to Orlando at the same time. She connected with me, and I asked if we could meet in person for breakfast. I had known her online for a number of years, but this was the first time we met in person. I got to meet her husband too!

Holly Rigsby, a Love Your Life Coach for moms, is an expert at this. She sat down and talked with me about how she shows gratitude for her clients. One of the most fun things she's done was meet up with her clients to go shopping and eat at The Cheesecake Factory! Everyone was waiting to see what Holly, who specializes in helping moms get fit, was going to order. Well, she ended up getting a couple glasses of wine, one of the biggest meals on the menu with meat on the bone, and—of course—cheesecake!

She treated this meetup as if she were hanging out with friends, showing them who she really was. This was about friends hanging out with friends—not a business owner hanging out with clients.

If you treat your clients like friends and family and allow them to see your authentic and true self, they will be with you for a long time.

TIP #13

Help Your Clients Learn Something New

Regularly offer trainings or classes for your clients and customers. Recently, The Body Shaping Company, a gym out in Denver where I do some personal training, had a vision board party at the beginning of the year. They brought in a guest speaker to talk about the power of creating a vision board to help you reach your goals and then everyone made their own vision board. The gym provided wine and snacks. It's these little things that will help your business create a more family-like atmosphere and improve retention.

Help Scout had another good example of this:

> *Let's say you own a coffee shop. How cool would it be to hold regular events where you bring in experts to talk about coffee and do free tastings? The more educated your customers become, the more they will*

appreciate coffee, thus the more valuable they are to your business.[10]

If you run on online business, you can offer free webinars or coaching to help your clients get more out of your product or service.

---

10   Help Scout, "25 Ways to Thank Your Customers," accessed Aug. 21, 2018, https://www.helpscout.net/25-ways-to-thank your-customers/.

TIP #14

Spotlight Clients and Customers on Social Media

Whether they're using Facebook, Instagram, or Snapchat, everyone is on social media these days. Call out customers on Facebook or Instagram to let them know how much they mean to you. Make it personal, be sincere, and leave them smiling. If they've gotten a result using your product or service, highlight that as well. And make sure you tag them, too, so their friends can see.

A great example of how I've done this is with my online fitness coaching program called Fit For Photos. It's a 9-week transformation program where all of the members commit to doing a professional photo shoot at the end of the 9 weeks.

Well, you can bet all of my Fit For Photos clients want to show off their professional photos on Facebook and Instagram after getting in the best shape of their life.

It's common for these photos to get over 100 likes and dozens of comments! All their friends want to know how they got such amazing results. And guess where they point to? Scott Colby and his Fit For Photos program. Instant social proof and referrals coming my way!

I'll spotlight them too! So many of my clients have lost weight, overcome addiction, gotten off medication, lowered their blood pressure, and more. I've interviewed several of them on my podcast, and they're always thrilled and flattered to be asked to talk about their transformation. With so much negativity on Facebook, why don't you turn your page into a place with inspiring stories that others look forward to reading?

I also feature clients in my private Fit For Photos group. After someone completes Fit For Photos, they get access to my Fit For Photos Warriors Facebook group (I call my Fit For Photos members Warriors), where all the members who completed the program hang out and get ongoing support.

Every Wednesday, I have a Warrior of the Week, where I feature one member, post their photos, and say something nice about them. It makes them feel special and appreciated.

Another way to profess your love for your customers

is to feature them on your website. This makes your customers feel valued and gives them a sense of pride in doing business with you.

TIP #15
Brand Yourself with Gratitude

Small acts of kindness can go a long way when it comes to building relationships. Let's face it: like it or not, we're right in the thick of a social media explosion. With Facebook, Instagram, and Snapchat—just to name a few platforms—we have more ways to communicate with people than ever before. Despite all of the political nonsense and complaining that goes on over social media, you can astutely use it to grow meaningful relationships.

Bardi Toto Drake, author of *The Power of Asking*, has used gratitude as the core of her marketing brand. When she began to use gratitude instead of "bragging and selling," her visibility advanced many times over, landing her on national television networks, television shows, and social media.

Cheryl Conner writes about Toto's approach in an article for Forbes:

Toto provides the following five mechanisms for expressing gratitude that have been most beneficial to her and that she recommends most highly to others, as follows:

1. **YouTube.** Share videos on various social networking sites that "speak" to your interests and principles, while also commenting to express your appreciation of their content and their value to you.

2. **Twitter.** Twitter provides the ideal opportunity to show gratitude for someone's remark by retweeting it ... "A retweet is a recognition of someone's value to you. That's a form of thanks," Toto says.

3. **Facebook Live.** You can comment and share someone's Facebook Live video, Toto says. "I have made a Facebook Live video sharing a business, book review as well as a testimony about another person or business while tagging them in the Facebook Live Video," she suggests.

4. **LinkedIn.** The very best way to express gratitude on LinkedIn is to recommend someone, congratulate them on their job anniversary or endorse them for a particular skill. "It takes less than five minutes to do this and adds weight and credibility to their

profile," she says. "If a connection performs a great service for you ... write them a recommendation."

5. **Instagram.** Reposting pictures, sharing, liking, using #hashtags to acknowledge a company and following others on Instagram is a way to show gratitude for the information someone else has shared.[11]

11   Cheryl Conner, "How Gratitude Advances Marketing and Business," Forbes, Apr. 26, 2017, https://www.forbes.com/sites/cherylsnappconner/2017/04/26/how-gratitude-advances-marketing-and-business/ - 5d35c0f37d68.

TIP #16
Be Real

Perhaps nothing goes further in growing your relationships with your customers than being real! Sounds simple, doesn't it? Well, for some, it's not.

How many times on Facebook do we only see the "highlight reel" of someone's life? Everything seems perfect, right? And then the comparison game starts. People start comparing their sad life with your seemingly perfect life, and feel depressed.

As my friend and mentor Tony Grebmeier says: "Show the good, the bad, and the ugly. Own it! When you show that you struggle, your customers and clients will actually appreciate it. As a professional in the fitness industry, I've shared photos of me eating pizza and cake and other junk food. And I've received comments from my clients that they appreciate seeing that I'm human—that I'm not perfect. Coaches, teachers, doctors, and other professionals are human. They're not perfect. They make mistakes. They own up to those mistakes. Be authentic, and your customers will relate to you even more. A great way to do this is to share personal stories on your public platform, good and bad."

I especially struggle with my sweet tooth. When it comes down to it, I guess I have a sugar addiction. A few years ago, I decided to write about "My Scary Doctor's Visit" on my blog. Here's what I wrote:

October was a busy month of new happenings, including a rare doctor's visit!

That's right. I rarely go to the doctor (I'm afraid of them), but a few weeks ago, I needed to. You see, last October, I got my blood work done, and everything looked good except my Testosterone level. It was lower than normal.

When my doctor called me with the test results last year, he wanted me to come back and get retested to make sure the number was correct. Well, being a guy that is afraid of needles, I never went back.

So you're probably wondering why I decided to go get re-tested this October. Well, there are days that I feel like I'm lacking energy, and I was wondering if low Testosterone had anything to do with that. If it did,

I wanted to possibly get treated for it so I could feel better.

So I scheduled a doctor's visit in early October. I had to choose a new doctor because I had a new insurance plan. And he decided to do all sorts of tests on me—cholesterol, blood sugar, liver, kidneys, and thyroid.

When I got the test results a few days later, my Testosterone was normal, as was everything else, except for my blood sugar. It came back a little high.

Much to my surprise, the doctor recommended that I lose 10–15 pounds. Now, I know that on the day of my doctor's visit, I wasn't at my fittest, but I had still been working out. They weighed me in at 201 pounds (with my clothes and shoes on). And this was the heaviest I've ever weighed. But being 6'1", I was surprised at the recommendation to lose weight.

Now here's where I have to admit something: When I'm not training for a specific purpose, like a photo shoot, my sweet tooth still gets the best of me. In fact, there are days where I'd eat some candy, some ice-cream and sometimes even a pastry. And I'm talking big servings of each of these, which I know could equate to hundreds of grams of sugar.

So if anything, my sugar intake is too high. Even though the doctor didn't recommend I eliminate all sugar, that's what I've chosen to do—I've eliminated all processed sugar from my diet. To be frank with you, his diagnosis scared the heck out of me. It sounded like I might be close to having diabetes.

I always tell my clients to come up with a big WHY they want to achieve a particular goal. Well I now had my big why! Giving up sweets, especially chocolate, has always been a challenge for me. Not anymore. I've got that blood test result in the back of my mind, and that's my big WHY.

I ate no candy on Halloween for the first time ever!

I also borrowed a scale, and even though I'm not a big believer in weighing yourself, I am keeping an eye on my weight. My doctor wants to check my blood sugar in six months, and as of writing this post, my weight is down to 187 (no clothes or shoes).

Besides giving up processed sugar, I've also made a couple other dietary changes in hopes that it will help my energy level. I've given up red meat (which I used to do a long time ago) and I drink a green smoothie every day. All 3 of these dietary changes have led to higher energy, and I'm feeling a lot better.

Here are a few of the comments I received from friends and clients in response to that post:

Peg said, "Thanks for the transparency and the inspiration!"

From Christy: "Scott, I love your constant drive for improvement. You are motivating me too!"

And my friend Terry commented, "Really appreciate your honesty, Scott! I wish you success in getting your health back to where you want it to be…life is an ongoing learning process, and I have learned a great deal working with you these past few years."

Remember, people do business with people they know, like, and trust. And there's no better way to have people know, like, and trust you than to be vulnerable, open up, and share your story.

TIP #17
Leave Reviews

Customer reviews lend credibility to your product or service. When prospects come to your website and they see that real people use your products and have had good things to say about your offerings, they're more likely to buy from you.

Why not lead the way and start leaving reviews for different people and businesses, rather than asking for them? Start leaving reviews for authors whose books you've read (Amazon and Goodreads are great places to start). Review podcasts you love (you can start with iTunes). And leave positive feedback about local businesses where you've had a good experience—think of doctors, dentists, veterinarians, real estate agents, etc. (you can do this on Yelp, Google, or Facebook).

By leaving reviews, you are providing goodwill and you'll begin to get noticed. When you leave reviews, you'll have a better chance of receiving reviews for your business.

If your business is receiving reviews, make sure you respond to them—both the positive and negative. I'm sure you understand the importance of responding to the negative reviews. It shows the unhappy customer (and the whole world) that you care about them and want to do what you can to make things right. Don't be defensive. Be empathetic and seek to understand their point of view. Remember, anyone and everyone will be able to see your response.

You should also respond to positive reviews. Positive reviews show who your fans are. They are promoters of your business—the ones that will tell their friends about you. A person who leaves a positive review for your business is a customer who will come back again. Show your appreciation by responding to them and acknowledging them.

Thank the reviewer and make it personal. Make sure you do it in a timely manner. If you let a review sit for months without responding, it looks like you don't care. Keep your response short, personal, and authentic. Say something specific about the review so the reviewer knows it's not just a copy-and-paste response. You can even ask them to take further action, such as telling their friends about you or signing up for another appointment.

While you're at it, share your positive reviews with the

world. For example, if you got a Google review, take a screenshot and share it on Facebook. That just may be the thing that a prospect needs to see to start buying your products or services.

TIP #18
Always Provide Outstanding Customer Service

Another way to get great reviews is to provide outstanding customer service.

It's kind of a shame that I have to make this a tip, but great customer service isn't always a given. How many times do we hear stories of poor or rude service? Unfortunately, it happens too often. And it sucks when we call a company, only to have to go through a robotic menu to get connected to the right person—only to be put on hold for 30 minutes. Kind of makes you feel like a number and not like a human.

Nothing says thanks for your business better than a friendly, informed service representative. It's uncanny how thrilled customers are when a real human answers the phone and doesn't read from a script.

Zappos has built their brand on focusing on the customer experience and letting their team members handle customer situations the way they see fit. Their CEO, Tony Hsieh, has literally written the book on delivering world-class customer service. And the stories of just how far they will go to make a customer happy are legendary.

One of the most famous Zappos customer support stories happened in December 2012 and set the record for being the longest customer support call ever. It lasted 10 hours and 29 minutes!

What the Zappos representative and the caller discussed for over 10 hours will remain a curious case to the rest of us (reports said they were talking about what it's like to live in Las Vegas). What we know for sure is that the 10-hour phone call resulted in a sale of a pair of Ugg boots, a world record, and a story that will be told for years to come.[12]

Give your customers other options on how to contact you besides calling your phone. Most people think that's a hassle these days, even if they're not put on

12   Caroline Fairchild, "Zappos' 10-Hour Long Customer Service Call Sets Record," HuffPost, updated Dec. 21, 2012, https://www.huffingtonpost.com/2012/12/21/zappos-10-hour-call_n_2345467.html.

hold for 30 minutes and forced to listen to awful music. Facebook Messenger can be used as a support tool for your customers to be able to get in touch with you. Companies such as Lowe's, Marriott, and Wells Fargo are taking service queries, payments, and even scheduling deliveries over iMessage. WhatsApp is used by over 3 million businesses aiming to offer better customer support over chat. You can also use Twitter to receive and respond to customers' direct messages. Customers love being able to use one of these platforms to get their questions answered or cancel a subscription.[13]

Want another simple tip to providing good customer support? You'll remember our friend Doug Spurling, the gym owner in Maine, when we talked about thank you cards. Doug's simple suggestion for providing outstanding customer service is to know your customer's name and repeat it 1,000 times. Then repeat it another 1,000 times.

As humans, our name is the word we like to hear the most. Think about your day-to-day life and how many businesses you walk into where you're not greeted by

---

13   Geoffrey Fowler, "Want better customer service? Don't call. Text." Washington Post, Aug. 9, 2018, https://www. washingtonpost.com/technology/2018/08/09/want-better-customer-service-dont-call-text/?utm_term=.2908f64e98c7.

your first name. If you walk into a coffee shop, very few baristas remember you by your first name. And if they do, chances are you're going to be a repeat customer. So greeting every single client or customer by their first name is a great tip to providing outstanding customer service.

TIP #19

Send Flowers

Send flowers or balloons to your best customers at their workplace—just because. You don't need a specific reason. It will brighten their day, and all of their coworkers will want to know where they came from. Make it a true celebration.

Representing your business, you're doing this to show true, genuine appreciation for your client while fostering human connection. This will also be great exposure for you and your business! Think about it: If you receive flowers at work, all of your coworkers will ask who sent them to you. If you tell everyone that your personal trainer sent them, it creates instant exposure for your trainer's fitness business and might even generate a new referral.

Sending flowers can be a versatile tool. "Banks are increasingly trying to forge a human connection with customers through what they call a 'surprise and delight' customer experience strategy. This means empowering customer service agents to go the extra mile to make a connection with the customer," explains Suman Bhattacharyya in an article on Tearsheet. The article goes on to describe the heartwarming story of a Capital One agent who went the extra mile for a customer:

> *Capital One customer and Pittsburgh resident Christina Grady, who was going through a difficult time after a breakup, phoned Capital One's call center last year after her credit card was shut down due to suspicious activity. Tonya, the customer service agent, did more than just reactivate the card. She gave Grady miles to use on a vacation and sent flowers. Grady posted her story on Facebook, and it went viral on social media. Tonya and Grady met for the first time as guests on Ellen DeGeneres' show.*[14]

With a little extra effort, Tanya helped a customer down on her luck and drew nationwide attention to the company. That's the power of great customer service! It really does pay in the long run.

---

14   Suman Bhattacharyya, "Send flowers: How banks are wooing customers with personal gifts," Tearsheet, July 20, 2017, http://www.tearsheet.co/modern-banking-experience/send-flowers-how-banks-are-wooing-customers-with-personal-gifts.

TIP #20

Make Your Customer Feel Special When You Ship Your Product

Nowadays, unboxing an order is an experience. You can ship your product in a plain brown box, or you can spruce it up. The extra effort is bound to make your customer feel special when they open it. Remember Stephanie Jones, author of *The Giving Challenge*? Stephanie illustrates a perfect example of this when shipping books to her clients.

She packages her book in a bright and colorful pink package. And instead of just writing the customer's name on the front, she writes "The Amazing" or "The Fabulous" before his or her name.

She signs every book and includes a bookmark and a personalized note with every package. Stephanie said she never realized what a gift it was to customers to

The Grateful Entrepreneur

go the extra mile in personalizing and beautifying their package. She was just trying to do something special.

But then one day a customer who had ordered her book took pictures of all those different things that Stephanie did when shipping the book (the packaging, the bookmark, the note), posted them on social media, and then wrote how each of those pieces made her feel. None of these things cost Stephanie very much—her bookmarks are pennies on the dollar, and the packaging is the same as what she would pay for boring packaging. But it's all these little things that make your customer feel special, like they're more than a number. So now you're not just shipping your product, you're also taking the time to let your customer know you care about them.

TIP #21
Say Happy Birthday

Send out birthday cards to every team member and customer on their birthday! If you're connected to your customers on Facebook, the platform lets you know when it's their birthday. It's a cinch to post "Happy Birthday" on their timeline. But hundreds of other people are doing the same thing. Too bad your message won't stand out.

Recently, I read about a CEO named Sheldon Yellen who handwrites 8,000 birthday cards a year for all his employees—with personalized comments relevant to each person! In addition, when he hears about random acts of kindness in the workplace, he sends a thank you note to the individual letting them know their efforts didn't go unnoticed.

These gestures helped Sheldon grow a billion-dollar disaster relief and property restoration company. Chris Weller told the story in an article for Business Insider:

Yellen said he started writing the birthday cards after he was hired by his brother-in-law, since many of the employees at the time felt he was being given special treatment. If nothing else, the birthday cards would encourage people to stop by his desk, he thought.

"And it worked," he previously told Business Insider. "It got people talking, we started to communicate more, and I like to think it helped me earn respect within the company."[15]

In order to get so many cards written, Yellen keeps a stack with him as he travels. He'll knock out a few here and there in his free time or during a long flight. Yellen reports that the gesture has had an influence on the atmosphere of the company over time. Because people feel appreciated, they're bringing more compassion into the workplace.

Yellen got the ultimate surprise on his birthday—all of his employees gave him a birthday card. That's 8,000 cards he received!

"To every single one of BELFOR's employees, I can't

---

15   Chris Weller, "A CEO who writes 8,000 employee birthday cards a year just got the ultimate 'thank you'," Business Insider, Jan. 18, 2018, http://www.businessinsider.com/ceo-writes-8000-birthday-cards-a-year-gets-ultimate-thank you-2018-1.

thank you enough for your birthday wishes and for your tireless, compassionate dedication to our customers," Yellen said in a statement. "I'm looking forward to reading each and every card!"[16]

A simple card can make a big impression! I remember when I bought my first car in Fairfax, Virginia: a 1992 Honda Accord. For years, I received a birthday card in the mail from the dealer who sold me the car. You can bet I would have bought my next car from her had I not moved to Dallas!

Do's and Don'ts of Sending Birthday Cards:

- Set up a system of reminders for your customers' birthdays. Punchbowl is a great online resource to help you get started.

- Create pockets of time for you to handwrite cards. Just like Yellen used his down time on a plane to get a stack done, you can find space a couple times during the week or month to get them written.

- Don't put your business cards inside a birthday card you're sending to a client. How does it feel when you receive a birthday card and a business card falls out of it?

---

16   Weller, Business Insider.

TIP #22

Take Your Clients out for Lunch or Dinner on Their Birthday

Want to take your clients' birthday celebration to the next level? Call up your client who is celebrating their birthday in the upcoming month and invite them to lunch or dinner. You could reach out and say, "I want to thank you for all the ways you have supported me this year by taking you out on your birthday. I would love to take you to your favorite restaurant. It's on me!"

Many people are too busy for coffee dates in the middle of the day, but taking someone out to a dinner at their favorite restaurant is an unexpected treat that will definitely make you stand out.

Encourage them to bring three of their friends along. What client would not respond to such warmth and gratitude?

At the meal, don't talk about business. And don't check your phone. How rude is that? We've all seen that table of people at a restaurant where no one is talking, and everyone is checking their phone.

Focus on the people in front of you. Connect with them on a personal level. You may learn something new about them, and you'll have the opportunity to share more about yourself. And if some of their friends come along, you have the added bonus of an instant referral opportunity.

Think what this strategy can do for client retention and new referrals. Gratitude Marketing shares a story about a financial advisor executing this strategy:

> *It was not unusual for his clients to invite the same three friends to join them for lunch from year to year. This allowed the advisor the opportunity to get to know the friends prior to taking them on as clients. Once the friends became clients, he invited them to lunch on their birthdays with the same stipulation that they bring three of their friends along. Each year, as the candles increased, so did the fond memories.*[17]

17   "How one simple idea nurtures referrals year in and year out," Gratitude Marketing, Sept. 27, 2016, https://gratitudemarketingbook.com/one-simple-idea-nurtures-referrals-year-year/.

TIP #23
Use Client Gratitude Videos

Genuine customer gratitude builds trust and inspires sales. Authentically capture your customers' buying experience on video as a tool for helping prospective customers feel more comfortable purchasing from you.

Yasmin Nguyen talked about this idea in The Grateful Entrepreneur Summit. He broke it down into simple terms when he shared a story about selling Girl Scout Cookies. I'll let Yasmin tell the story in his own words:

About six years ago, I was speaking at a non-profit technology conference in Washington, DC, where I stayed with my friends Neil and Heather. Now Neil and Heather had this amazing 10-year-old daughter named Kendall. And every morning when we would sit down and have breakfast together, Kendall would just light up the room with her energy and her curiosity. Seeing how happy and positive she was made a great start to the day! On my third and final day there, Kendall was really quiet and she just kept herself.

As she was looking down at her bowl of cereal, I said, "Hey, Kendall. What's going on? You seem different today."

She said, "Yeah, well, I have to go sell Girl Scout Cookies."

"What's wrong with that? People love cookies."

She's like, "Yeah, but every time I go out ask someone if they want to buy a box of cookies, I get rejected and that doesn't feel good."

"Oh, Kendall, I totally understand," I said. "I've been rejected so many times, and you're right. It doesn't feel good…Kendall, how much are your cookies?"

"They're four dollars a box," she said.

So I reached in my wallet. I pulled out $20. I gave it to her, and I said, "Hey, why don't you give me five boxes?"

"Really?"

"Yeah," I said. "Now, here's the thing, Kendall. I don't eat cookies myself, so I want you to take those five boxes and give them to five people you've never met before."

All of a sudden her eyes lit up. She leapt out of her chair. She ran to her mom and said, "Mom, guess what? We get to give cookies away."

Her excitement changed just like that.

I said, "Now, Kendall, here's the reason I want you to do that: I want you to know what it's like to just make someone's day. I want you to see and hear and just feel their appreciation. I want you to do that five times so you really know what that's like. Then when you're out there and you're selling cookies, try this: Instead of asking someone if they want to buy cookies, ask them, "Hey, is there someone in your life that you really care about? Because I'd like to help you make their day by giving them a box of cookies."

What we're doing is taking this experience that we're stressed about, in this case selling, and instead of trying to convince someone to do something, like buy your product, now we're creating an opportunity for them to give.

Yasmin's message of gratitude-inspired selling is all about helping someone see what's possible through our customer stories. This builds trust and connection with prospective clients.

But too often we're approaching these customer stories or case studies experiences by trying to do a "testimonial." When we ask a customer to do a testimonial for us, it comes across as asking them for a favor, which creates an energy of it being about you and trying to prove yourself.

Whereas, if you approach it from a gratitude-inspired selling approach, you're really appreciating someone that you've served well, and you're inviting them to share their story. Have them share their journey and their decision-making process. Ultimately, that creates a space for them to share their gratitude for how you've served them or helped them. Now we have an opportunity to deepen that connection.

It's giving them a box of cookies to pass along to someone else.

A company called Vibrance Global, which Yasmin runs, does this well. They help businesses produce customer gratitude videos to build that trust. Their website explains:

> The "Gratitude Inspired Sales™" approach is designed to leverage the emotional connection with and influence of a peer to elevate trust with the seller. "Buyer Trust" is a natural byproduct of sharing "Customer

Gratitude". More effective than written testimonials for high-risk purchases, these Customer Gratitude Videos give the buyer an authentic experience of what it's like to momentarily be a customer. As a result, this trust reduces buyer's risk and this accelerates the sales process.[18]

If your client is nervous on camera, a great way to put them at ease is to start off with gratitude. Start off by telling your client how much you appreciate them, how thoughtful they are, how committed they are, and what of a difference they've made. By doing that right at the beginning of the conversation, you help them release any anxiety and stress associated with a need to perform. They receive your gratitude, and now they're ready to reciprocate by sharing their amazing, authentic experience.

---

18   http://www.vibranceglobal.com.

TIP #24
Create Personal Thank You Videos

Most of us have email autoresponder messages set to thank our customers for a purchase. It's the same email that goes out to everyone. Set yourself apart by taking 60 seconds to create a personalized video thanking your customer for purchasing your product or service. That short amount of time will make a world of difference in setting you and your business apart. I did this for a while with all my Fit For Photos clients, and they truly appreciated it.

Once, when I was shopping for a new virtual CFO, I was interviewing a Profit First Professional, Joanne, in nearby Parker, Colorado. Mike Michalowicz, author of *Profit First*, recorded a personal video for me, just to say that he hoped I worked with Joanne and that he would be available to answer any questions. It was quite a thrill to get that personal video. It made such an impression on me that I did hire Joanne to be my virtual CFO!

There are tools you can use to make this process easier. Bonjoro is a video email app that helps you delight your customers from day one, helping you create a human connection by sending a personal onboarding video right to your customer's inbox. You'll retain more customers because they will feel like more than just a number. By showing them love with these personal videos, you'll elevate your relationships with them, and they will stick around.

BombBomb is a company that does something similar. They help you rehumanize your communication with simple videos to build trust and convert leads.

TIP #25
Get on the Phone

This one is similar to the previous tip on creating personal thank you videos. Pick up the phone and make gratitude phone calls. An ever-growing number of social media platforms makes the Internet a very crowded place; sometimes it's difficult to make your voice heard among the crowd. That's why it's good to go old school sometimes with a phone call.

John Lee Dumas from EOFire makes a personal call to every person who joins his membership program, Podcasters' Paradise. John is very busy running a successful business with the help of Kate Erickson. But business is about relationships, so they both make the time to care for their customers. You can't "scale" human relationships, and you shouldn't even try. Plus, calling people on the phone to thank them helps you stand apart because no one is doing it. Some of John's customers are so impressed by the personal phone calls and videos they receive from him that they talk about it on social media. More exposure for John and his business!

Not every phone call with your clients and customers needs to be about business, either. Remember, your business is about building relationships and treating your customers like people, not dollar signs.

That's right—pick up the phone and call your customers just to check up on them. See how things are going in their life. Ask if there is anything you can do to help them. This one simple gesture of a personal phone call will go a long way to cultivating relationships in your business.

My friend and mentor Tony Grebmeier is really good at this. He'll call or text me just to see how I'm doing, ask me about my relationships, and see if I need anything from him. If it's a call, it takes about 5 minutes. If it's a text, it's even quicker.

I remember my first mentor, Ryan Lee, would do the same thing. He would just call me out of the blue. This was before the days of Facebook and Instagram. I remember being so excited (and surprised) when his name showed up on my cell phone. That little gesture is one of the things that has kept me loyal to learning from Ryan for over 15 years now.

TIP #26

Cultivate Relationships and Community in a Digital World

You might remember Holly Rigsby, a Love Your Life Coach for moms, from an earlier tip. When I interviewed Holly for The Grateful Entrepreneur Summit, she shared some great tips for cultivating relationships in a digital world.

For Holly, it boils down to how she wants someone to feel after their first interaction with her. She signs her emails "Your friend and coach" because she wants her customers and prospects to know she's there for them— not only to help solve their problem, but also as a friend. She's not just selling them a program and saying, "Good luck." She's there for the long haul as a trusted coach that moms can relate to.

She keeps her community small and goes deeper into the relationships because then she gets to go on the journey with these moms. This also allows her to reply to every Facebook comment and answer every email. Every time she does this, Holly is building more trust, and her customers stick around longer and buy more from her.

Holly likes sending her clients handwritten thank you notes. Her sister once said that getting "a handwritten note is like receiving a smile in your mailbox." This is so true! And Holly wants to put a smile on every client's face. She also pays attention to the little details of a customer's life. If a client has a small win or is going through a rough time, she includes something special to go along with the note.

Holly suggests making your handwritten notes stand out. For example, she buys boxes of quote cards from bookstores and writes a little message on each card she sends to clients. Or she might send a quote poster she finds at Hobby Lobby—something the client can frame—and include a note that says, "Hey, I'm just thinking about you." The message of the poster might relate to a challenge the client is facing or a win she just achieved. Her clients love these! It's the kind of gift they display so they can see it all the time. And you can bet they think of Holly every time they look at it.

Another of Holly's ideas is to make videos for her clients to watch on Facebook. A video creates an instant connection and builds trust. Videos also allow you to highlight your clients with stories. Storytelling helps spark hope in other people going through the same challenges. Facebook live is a great way to provide instant connection. You can ask your clients questions and provide feedback for them.

People want to be seen and heard. It's as simple as acknowledging them.

Alicia Streger, another of the professionals I interviewed for The Grateful Entrepreneur Summit, has done a great job cultivating relationships in her Facebook group, Fitness Business Freedom Formula. She created the group as a place for fitness professionals and health coaches to connect and communicate. Being an entre-preneur can be a lonely game. A lot of us feel isolated working behind our computers, so it's nice to have a place to build genuine connections with like-minded professionals. Alicia gives away a lot of free content on the page to help people in their businesses. And the group is a great support structure for encouragement and celebration.

Giving away content is a form of gratitude. How has that helped Alicia grow her business? Most of the people who have signed up for Alicia's high-level coaching program say they got to know her through the Facebook group.

She gives away content, answers questions, engages the members, and shows up daily.

Alicia's #1 content strategy for getting engagement in her Facebook group is doing weekly challenges where the winner gets a prize. One of my favorite weekly challenges Alicia did was a thank you card challenge: write 5 random cards to clients just to show you appreciate them. The Facebook group members had to take a picture of the 5 cards they wrote and post it in the comments. At the end of the week, Alicia drew a random winner to receive a cool prize.

Can you see Alicia's approach working for your business? How might you benefit from cultivating a sense of community in your professional sphere of influence?

TIP #27

Run Your Business Like a Relationship

Honorée Corder's book *Business Dating* explores the idea of treating your business relationships like your personal relationships. She shared some of her best ideas with us during The Grateful Entrepreneur Summit.

Her first point? You wouldn't propose on a first date, right? Well, in the same way, you shouldn't be asking for a sale during your first interaction with a prospect. Be openly available to other people and be authentic. Be willing to share of yourself, and be willing to be less than perfect. Playing the long game means recognizing that people are people—not dollar signs. They have their own interests and priorities. This means figuring out who and what those priorities are, learning about their goals, and acknowledging the fact that this prospective client is a person. Out of that realization, you can connect with them on a personal level.

You can send someone a thank you note for doing

something for you, such as being on your podcast. Be sure to personalize it to make it more meaningful. How do you personalize a note to a client? You have to take time to learn about them first. Is she married? Is he involved with someone? Do they have children? What's their business or career about? What is he looking for? When is her birthday? Once you have this type of personal information, you can even go another level deeper. If the client has a business, you can learn about it too. What are they looking for most in their business? Who do they want to meet? Or who do they need on their team that they don't already have? You can be a connector and introduce them to the right people to help them grow their business.

The more you can learn about this client, the more you can personalize the relationship. Can you see how, when the time comes for the prospect to invest, your personal relationship makes you stand out from your competitors in the customer's mind? They're much more likely to do business with the person who has taken the time to build a relationship with them.

Honorée suggested another simple way to start building that relationship with people is to ask: What do you need next in your life or in your business? Ultimately, when you meet someone for the first time, you're on opposite sides of the trust bridge, as Honorée puts it. They don't know, like, or trust you yet. The way to get them on your side of the trust bridge so they will ultimately buy from you is to build that personal relationship with them.

You just keep touching someone over and over again with phone calls, visits, notes, emails, gifts of gratitude, and acknowledgment until you get to the other side of the trust bridge. Make sure you also look for ways to add value to other people that has absolutely nothing to do with what you're selling. Maybe you're bringing soup to someone because they're sick. That's being kind. That's being a friend and treating the other person like a human. That's what builds the relationship.

Pat Rigsby is an expert at this approach. Pat has been a mentor and coach of mine for over a decade. He consults with entrepreneurs, coaching them to create their ideal business. One of the first lessons I learned from Pat was to treat my prospects and customers like people—not a transaction.

I sat down and interviewed Pat for The Grateful Entrepreneur Summit. Here were some of the big takeaways:

- When we think about business, it should start at the person level, not the product level. Typically when somebody's buying something, they have a problem they're trying to solve. We help them escape from that problem and arrive at a solution.

- This comes from building a relationship with a client. Even if it's a short-term relationship. We start by asking questions: How can I help? What do you need? What kind of problem are you trying to solve? By creating meaningful pathways of communication, we open the door for customers to know us, like us, and trust us to provide the solution.

- And then we want to build a relationship with them, so they can trust us, and in an ongoing way. If they feel valued and important—seen as a person instead of a dollar sign—it's going to allow us to serve our customers in an ongoing way. That creates a healthier, more sustainable business.

- A great way to cultivate those relationships is through personal interactions. Send clients a handwritten note, make a phone call, check in with a text message, schedule a video chat. These are all ways to make your customers feel valued, heard, and important.

- If you treat your prospects like clients, and your clients like family, you'll be separating yourself from the crowd. Not many businesses are doing this. Do a good job of showing appreciation and gratitude. Clients will remember you and refer other customers to you.

There's always a time and a place to ask for business, but when you're trying to mix it with appreciation and gratitude, it just comes across as being insincere and disingenuous. Show authentic appreciation and gratitude, and trust that it will come back to you when the time is right.

As Maya Angelou put it, "People will forget what you said, people will forget what you did, but people will never forget how you made them feel."[19]

---

19   "Maya Angelou Quotes," Goodreads, accessed August 22, 2018, https://www.goodreads.com/quotes/5934-i-ve-learned-that-people-will-forget-what-you-said-people.

TIP #28
Appreciate Employees

Most people in the workplace don't feel appreciated or valued. As a result, they don't feel grateful for their job or their boss. Over time this can create a lack of morale and contribute to low motivation. It also impacts the customer experience, team spirit, and organizational effectiveness.

I remember feeling this way during my first job out of graduate school. I took a 9-month research internship position at a sports medicine clinic in Vail, Colorado. The whole time, something felt a little bit off.

One day I had a private meeting with my supervisor to discuss what I could be doing better, or how I didn't do something the right way. There was no mention of anything good I had done.

I walked out of that meeting with my shoulders slumped and my head down.

I thought to myself, *Is this what the working world is like? There's no way I can endure this for 40+ years until I retire.*

That experience was a huge catalyst for me eventually starting my own business.

Is this happening in your business?

I interviewed Dr. Paul White, co-author of *The 5 Languages of Appreciation in the Workplace.* He said research shows that 79% of people who leave a job voluntarily site a lack of appreciation as one of the major reasons for leaving. And despite 90% of companies in the United States having some form of employee recognition program, 65% of workers report they haven't received any recognition for doing a good job in the past year.

Something's not adding up.

Now, imagine if you could turn that around. What would the professional culture of your organization look like if it were full of employees who felt appreciated, recognized, and motivated to contribute to the success of the team? Can you feel the boost in morale? This starts with appreciating your employees on a regular basis. Your employees will also stay longer, work harder, and have a stake in the success of your organization. Best of all, this will save you money in the long run!

And it's not enough to just say, "Good job."

It turns out there are 5 languages of appreciation in the workplace, which are written about extensively in Dr. White's book. It's a spinoff of Gary Chapman's wildly popular book *The 5 Love Languages*.

The thing employees want most is a sense of being valued by both supervisors AND coworkers. They want to know that what they're doing matters. They want to know *they* matter. If not, the motivation wanes over time.

The #1 factor in job satisfaction is not the amount of pay but whether the individual feels appreciated and valued for the work they do. Oftentimes, there is a discrepancy between what leadership thinks is happening and how employees feel.

Each of us likes to feel appreciated in a certain way. Let's explore the 5 languages in more detail.

The 5 Languages of Appreciation:

1. **Words of affirmation.** The first and most common is words of affirmation. Research suggests that 46% of the workforce prefer words. This can be spoken

or written, but employees need to be affirmed. The more specific you can be, the better. Polling data shows that people don't want to hear "Good job" because it's just too general. Here's a better alternative: "Hey, Scott, thanks for showing up on time so I don't have to worry about somebody being here to greet our customers and clients." So you want to be very specific and make that person feel seen and appreciated.

2. **Quality time.** People are busy, but one of the things Dr. White tells leaders is just because your colleague or coworker wants quality time doesn't mean they want time with you. You may be great, you may be super, but more and more people, especially younger workers, like to hang out with their colleagues. So they will all go out to lunch or go out after work. When they're included, they feel valued.

3. **Acts of service.** People who prefer acts of service have the mind-set that words are cheap. *Don't tell me you value me. Show me.* Probably the best example of this is when you've got a time-sensitive project you're really pushing to get done. The person who prefers acts of service might appreciate having someone step in to help. You could bring

that person lunch, answer their calls for them, or help them with their project.

4. **Tangible gifts.** This doesn't have to be big. It could be a cup of coffee, donuts, or a favorite pizza. It's showing that you're paying attention and getting to know them and what they like.

5. **Physical touch.** Be careful with this one. This is really about spontaneous celebration. It's a high five when you finish a project, a fist bump when you solve a problem, a congratulatory handshake when you make a sale.

If you're not used to giving appreciation in the workplace, the easiest place to start is with words because we know that you're going to have almost a 50% chance of hitting the mark. Do it privately and be specific. People like to hear their name. If you're writing a note, spell their name correctly. That's important.

The biggest hurdle is just to start somewhere with somebody. If you wait for perfect conditions, it rarely happens. The easiest way to start is with somebody you work with day to day. Think about someone whose role directly affects your daily life. If this person didn't do his or her job, your life would be a lot tougher. You better make sure they know you value them. Otherwise, you might be at risk of losing them, and your life will become harder.

So start with the people you know—those who serve you and make life good for you. Just jot them a note or say a little brief something to them privately.

It's your job to learn the preferred language of appreciation for each of your team members then show them appreciation on a regular basis in their preferred language.

Can appreciation in the workplace help your bottom line?

According to Dr. White, staff turnover is the single largest non-productive cost to businesses! But when people feel valued and appreciated, we decrease the potential for turnover. First of all, conflicts that take up time and energy often go away. Happy employees are more willing to do what you ask, follow policies and procedures, and find solutions to problems in the workplace. All of these aspects contribute to you accomplishing the mission of your organization, serving your people well, and solving problems brought to you by clients and customers.

There is a big difference between employee recognition

programs and appreciating people in the workplace. Recognition really is designed to reward performance, and that's okay. But we're people. We're not just producers. We're not just work units. So, when we don't feel treated like a person, something is missing.

And that's really where appreciation fills the gap. Recognition focuses on performance. Appreciation focuses on the person.

TIP #29

Celebrate Employee Milestones with Gratitude

Celebrating employee milestones contributes to happiness in the workplace. This could be a work anniversary, a successful publication, a major deal—it could be any number of things. Of course, you can celebrate these milestones with a gift, flowers, or cake in the company break room, but I have a better idea!

There's a platform called Tribute that creates a video montage of employees telling a coworker why they're awesome. This is a guaranteed tearjerker! So, which gift is more meaningful—a gigantic cake that will leave you in a sugar coma, or a video montage with people expressing heartfelt appreciation and congratulations?

My online fitness company made a video like this for my sister, Jill! She worked with me for about 3 ½ years in a virtual position. So when she left, there was no office celebration with cakes and balloons because, well, there was no office. Instead, we used Tribute to collect videos from several of our fitness members thanking Jill and saying what they appreciated most about her. Tribute put all the videos into a montage, set it to music, and sent it to Jill. What a way to express gratitude!

The Tribute video we made for Jill is available online here if you want to see it for yourself:

www.tribute.co/jill-colby

TIP #30
Throw Welcome and Goodbye Parties

Throw welcome and goodbye parties to acknowledge team members or even clients. If someone joins your gym, for example, make a fuss over them and introduce them to everyone so they feel right at home. There's nothing worse than joining a new gym and attending your first workout class, only to stand there alone before the workout begins while everyone else talks to each other. If this happens, you'll probably feel alone and maybe even intimidated because you're not sure what to expect. This example hits close to home because it happened to me when I joined a gym.

As a result, I made sure to introduce new members when I ran bootcamp workouts in Dallas. It makes such a big difference!

If someone leaves, throw a goodbye party for them so they know they'll be missed. You could make a Tribute video like we talked about in the previous tip, have a potluck lunch, or even host a dinner or happy hour after work. Take it a step further and go around the room so each person can express gratitude for the person leaving. Writing a card to express heartfelt appreciation is another great way to send off your coworker or client in style.

TIP #31

Plan an Excursion

Organize a day off for your team. You can do a team-building scavenger hunt, go to a ball game, or even take a day trip somewhere.

Stacey Alcorn, CEO of LAER Realty Partners, organized a holiday shopping trip to New York City for her team. It was a 3 ½ hour bus trip each way, and she wasn't sure her sales agents and employees would be interested in this. But the bus trip sold out in less than 2 days! Getting out of town for the day to shop, eat, and have fun was exactly what her team wanted. This improves company culture and morale.

I love the idea of getting away from your work environment and taking your team somewhere they can bond. It's important not to make this a work trip, but rather a place where employees can relax, laugh, and get to know each other better on a personal level.

Another key goal is to help the team take a break from technology. When you get away from computer screens, smartphones, and the 24/7 "always on" attitude that so many of us live in, you really unplug and decompress. You'll find that your teammates come away with newfound creative inspiration, perspective, and personal growth.

Studies have shown that if you're stuck in a creative rut, one of the best ways out is to unplug and recharge. A study published in the journal *PLOS One*, shows that spending four nature-filled days, *away from electronic devices*, is linked to 50% higher scores on a test for creativity.[20]

Not only will an excursion like this improve company culture and morale, it will contribute to improved happiness, creativity, and problem-solving skills. Ultimately, it will lead to a better workplace with higher performance.

---

20   University of Utah, "Nature nurtures creativity," EurekAlert! Dec. 12, 2012, https://www.eurekalert.org/pub_releases/2012-12/uou-nnc120712.php.

TIP #32

Express Personal Gratitude Daily

Let's take a step back and talk about personal gratitude. Each day find something non-business related to be grateful for: your health, your family, or the roof over your head. Being a business owner has its ups and downs. There will be times when you want to give up. There will be times when you won't want to get out of bed. There will be times when you want other people to do the hard work.

Expressing gratitude daily can improve your mood and increase your happiness and optimism. It will help you complain less and look on the bright side of things. It will help you appreciate what you have. Cultivating a personal practice of gratitude can boost your motivation levels and increase your business performance.

Ultimately, it's essential to fuel your personal gratitude so you'll have a deep well to draw from in showing gratitude and appreciation to others.

The 3-1-3 System

Let me give you my 3-1-3 system for personal gratitude:

If you follow this daily, I truly believe it has the power to change your life and increase your business.

3—when you wake up on the morning, take out a journal and write down 3 things or people you're grateful for. Don't just say what they are, add WHY you're grateful for these 3 things. Really feel it, believe it, and live it.

1—In the evening, maybe when you've put away your work for the day, give thanks for one person who impacted you during the day. You might give thanks for the coworker who helped with a project, the spouse you woke up to this morning, or the barista who smiled at you in the coffee shop. Take this a step further by telling that person you are grateful for them and why. Even better, send them a handwritten thank you card.

3—Before you go to bed, list 3 wins from your day, big or small. We often beat ourselves up for our failures. I want you to go to bed in a celebratory mood. Writing down your 3 wins every night before bed will help with this. You'll be in a good mood when you shut off the lights.

And that's it! It's pretty simple stuff, but it requires a daily commitment to the habit.

Let me go back to my Guatemala story to help you understand the benefits of gratitude.

During my time in Guatemala, I became close with students and their parents. I was shocked by their overall positive demeanor. These families were all struggling in some way, yet they never failed to express pure, genuine appreciation for our efforts. Their attitude toward life seemed to emphasize gratitude and graciousness; it lacked the negativity so common to our American way of life. There was no sign of a grass-is-always-greener mind-set. They didn't seem to care about material possessions. They were content with what they had and thrilled with their new school.

Though the trip was one of the most fulfilling experiences of my life, it left me feeling conflicted when I returned home. I couldn't understand why the students and parents in Guatemala seemed so happy, despite having so little. By comparison, wealthy Americans struggle with contentment on a daily basis.

That's when it hit me: The difference is gratitude.

I started doing research on the mental effects of

expressing gratitude, hoping to better understand how to implement it within my own life.

According to leading gratitude researcher, Robert Emmons, the act of consciously expressing gratitude has been scientifically proven to increase happiness and decrease depression. It also:

- opens the door to more relationships,
- improves physical and psychological health,
- enhances empathy and reduces aggression,
- improves quality of sleep and self-esteem, and
- increases mental strength.

When you begin to practice personal gratitude on a regular basis, you will experience these positive effects. It can be truly life-changing for you.

It's never easy to begin a new daily habit, but these four tips can help get you started:

1. Start small.

Start small and practice the habit of writing one thing down that you're grateful for. Once that becomes a habit, you can build on my 3-1-3 system for personal gratitude.

2. Get your materials ready.

Writing gratitude involves a journal, or piece of paper and a pen. Have all of these out the evening before so you're ready to go the next day!

3. Figure out what time you'll write down your gratitude.

I love journaling gratitude as part of my morning routine. Expressing gratitude first thing in the morning improves my odds of getting it done.

As the day goes by, and other "stuff" gets in the way, writing in my gratitude journal becomes more difficult.

4. Practice habit stacking.

When creating this new habit, you'll have a better chance of sticking with it if you stack it on an existing habit. Perhaps you make coffee first thing each morning.

Making coffee can be the trigger to write in your gratitude journal. While you're sitting down enjoying that freshly brewed cup of coffee, put pen to paper and express gratitude.

TIP #33
Fuel Your Gratitude Habit

Once you've established a daily gratitude habit, as we discussed in the previous tip, be sure to fuel the habit. Even our most powerful routines can grow stale over time, so it's important to renew our passion and appreciation for them over time.

Remember Yasmin Nguyen? Yasmin talks about three different levels of gratitude.

Gratitude 1.0 is really about deepening a connection with ourselves. When we deepen our connection with ourselves, we're able to show up with more confidence and clarity.

Gratitude 2.0 is about deepening a connection with another person. How can we enhance that relationship with more trust and value?

Gratitude 3.0 is about creating an opportunity for others to witness a moment of gratitude and appreciation.

How can you inspire others to take action and practice showing gratitude? For example, in this book, I'm sharing different tools with you to add gratitude to your life and business. Hopefully, you'll come away inspired to spread more gratitude.

Yasmin likes the concept of a kick-ass jar as another way to integrate gratitude 1.0 into your life.

Have you ever struggled with self-doubt or just felt stuck in a rut?

Of course you have. We all have. But this is especially true for entrepreneurs. Running your own business is such a roller coaster ride. One day you're on top, ready to change the world. And the very next day, it can all come crashing down. Imposter syndrome sets in and you're riddled with worry, depression, and self-doubt. It's awful.

That's where the kick-ass jar comes in. Take a little tablet of sticky notes and carry it with you every day. When something positive happens, write it down, and put it in the kick-ass jar.

It can be anything—gaining a new client, having an inspiring conversation, feeling inspired by the scenery on a hike, receiving or writing a thank you card. Record every win from your day, no matter how big or small.

Then when you're having a rough day—and you WILL have rough days—take out a few of the sticky notes from the kick-ass jar and read them. This will provide an instant boost in confidence and self-esteem. In no time, you'll feel your kick-ass attitude returning.

What does this have to do with helping your business?

Think about it. Will you be able to serve your clients and customers better when you're down and depressed, or when you're excited, energized, and on top of the world?

It's pretty obvious when you think about it that way, right?

TIP #34

Go Complaint Free for 21 Days

Will Bowen's book, *A Complaint Free World,* challenges readers to go complaint free for 21 consecutive days. If you complain before 21 straight days are up, you go back to day one. It usually takes several months to complete this.

This is similar to expressing personal gratitude on a daily basis, like we talked about in the previous tip. You can't complain *and* be in a grateful state of mind at the same time. There's a lot of gossip that tends to go on in businesses. People complain about their bosses. Bosses complain about their employees. Team members complain about each other. This all leads to a toxic culture. It brings on negative emotions that can affect your energy levels and decrease performance.

According to Will Bowen, 78% of workers in the United States estimate wasting more than three to six hours every week listening to coworkers complain. For a small business with only 200 employees, that's $1.2 million every year in lost productivity alone.

One out of every 11 people quit their jobs because of complaining coworkers. And these are always the best employees because good people value organizational culture even more than money, opportunity, and recognition. Good people simply don't want to work in a nest of complainers, so they quit.

From this perspective, your biggest competitor is the time and effort your employees put into complaining, but you can change that! Complaint Free® Businesses enjoy greater creativity and collaboration, higher profits, lower turnover, and greater customer satisfaction.[21]

Pledge to go complaint free, and watch your business grow. Imagine if you ran a business where no one complained. Productivity and performance would soar through the roof!

---

21   For more, visit http://www.willbowen.com/complaintfree/

TIP #35

Start Your Meetings with Gratitude

Use this tip to cultivate a culture of gratitude in your workplace. In tip #32, we talked about expressing personal gratitude on a daily basis. We know that starting your day with gratitude can set the tone for a positive mind-set which leads to a positive day. The same idea applies to meetings. If you have team meetings where you discuss workplace problems, start your meetings off by going around the room and having each person share one thing they're grateful for.

Keep in mind, many people hate meetings. They may come into the meeting in the mood of their last phone call, email they read, or personal interaction they had. So why not get everyone engaged in the meeting from the outset by expressing gratitude, either personally or professionally? Try it, and I bet you'll find a little joy brought to your meetings.

Another great idea is to close your meeting with

gratitude. Take a minute before you wrap up your meetings and acknowledge people's contributions. Thank each person by name in a sincere and meaningful way. Try it for a few meetings. I can assure you, not only will your team notice and appreciate it, they will bring their very best to your next meeting and help make the time more productive and enjoyable.

Integrated Loyalty Systems uses this approach, which they've written about on their website:

> First, we go around the table and invite everyone to share any special news about themselves or their family with the team. It's totally voluntary so no one feels obligated to share. But often, we hear news about a fun family vacation, or an anniversary, or pictures from a child's winning soccer game. This only takes five or 10 minutes. It's a great ice-breaker and it allows us to get to know one another outside of our work roles.

> Still in "human" mode, we shift to kindness shout-outs. Basically, we open the floor for any team member to give a shout-out to any other team member for an act of kindness.

> This is where my team really shines. This is their chance to say thank you to a colleague for going above and

beyond on a project or task. It's great to hear them lift one another up and offer kudos for a job well done.

This can take another five or 10 minutes, which can sometimes cut into our "business" time—but it's worth it. The whole exercise helps build trust and camaraderie between and among our team members and it leaves us all with smiles as we transition into the business at hand.[22]

---

22   Jake Poore, "Showing Kindness and Gratitude in a Team Meeting—Here's How We Do It," accessed Aug. 24, 2018, https://www.wecreateloyalty.com/how-to-show-kindness-in-team-meetings/.

TIP #36
Give Back

Gratitude and giving back go hand in hand. If you REALLY want to create a culture of gratitude in your company, consider volunteering with your team. Some examples are: feeding the homeless, building a house through Habitat For Humanity, or hosting a fundraiser to raise proceeds for a specific charity. Get your customers and clients involved too!

I interviewed Yanik Silver, author of *Evolved Enterprise*. Yanik explained that an evolved enterprise is a company that has a greater impact, seeking a greater meaning and purpose to what they do. It starts with entrepreneurs discovering what they were designed for. What about you? What's your ultimate purpose? What can you uniquely put out into the world?

Yanik describes this concept as a system of concentric circles. The inner ring is the cause, your why. The next ring out is the creation of the products and services and how they're baked into the cause.

From there you move to the community ring—having customers who are just so excited to buy from you that they become advocates.

Finally, the outermost ring is the culture. How do you create a world-class culture with a big vision and core values that you instill throughout the organization?

Evolved Enterprise in Action

One way to give back is to have a 1: 1 giving model. TOMS shoes does this really well. For every pair of shoes sold, they give a pair of shoes to kids in need. Using this model, they've given away over 75 million pairs of shoes.

Bombas, a sock company, donates a pair of socks for every pair sold. They started by learning that socks are the most requested item in homeless shelters. They thought it would take them 10 years to donate a million pairs of socks. But using the evolved enterprise principles accelerated their growth, and it took them only two and half years to donate a million pairs!

FEED is another company doing this well. They sell

bags and feed the hungry. For example, some of the bags they sell provide 50 school meals to kids.

Elvis and Kresse is a company doing some great things. One day, the two designers were walking down the street and passed by a fire station where they saw an old fire hose waiting to be moved to a landfill. They had an aha moment. They started repurposing fire hoses into belts, iPad accessories and iPhone accessories, phone covers, keychain holders, etc. They donate 50% of their profits to charities that help firefighters. What an incredible circle of good they're creating!

Yanik talked about another model in our interview and in his book *Evolved Enterprise* that he calls Empowered Employment. In this model, companies work directly with underserved or marginalized communities for labor, creation, and design.[23]

Brewability Lab offers delicious craft beer in Denver and the surrounding area. They're a great example of the Empowered Employment model. They offer a dis-ability-friendly and blind-friendly bar, with a founding history of providing training, support, and entertainment for adults with disabilities by introducing them to the ever-growing industry of custom crafted beer.

---

23   Yanik Silver, Evolved Enterprise (Ideapress Publishing, 2017).

You can also have a portion of every sale go to a specific charity. When I started Say It With Gratitude, the cards were hand drawn by kids who had been impacted by a charity. Whenever we sold a pack of cards, we donated back to that charity. We ended up supporting charities that helped build schools in third world countries, fight hunger and cancer affecting children, as well as kids who had been abused or bullied.

The giving has to be sincere. And it should align with your overall company mission and values. Kentucky Fried Chicken got into a lot of trouble a couple of years back when they tried to do these pink buckets of chicken where fifty cents went to breast cancer research for each bucket sold. Corporate tried to make it work because KFC sells breasts of chicken and they were donating money to breast cancer research. But you could tell it was more about making them look good. In fact, there's research showing that fried food high in trans fats can cause cancer, so it really made very little sense. It sends a mixed message, says Barbara Brenner, executive director of Breast Cancer Action. "They are raising money for women's health by selling a product that's bad for your health ... it's hypocrisy."[24]

If you want to give back through your business, a company that can facilitate it is B1G1.com. B1G1 has partnered with over 500 carefully screened high-impact projects—everything from providing clean water to educating kids. You then choose how you want to give.

For example, if you run a coffee shop, you can set it up so that every time a customer purchases a coffee, a child in Tanzania gets access to clean drinking water. Using B1G1, you set up a giving story where you link a business activity to a particular project you'd like to give to.

Another thing B1G1 allows businesses to use are gratitude certificates. Giving gratitude certificates to your customers is perfect for sharing the story of your giving and to personally thank and delight your customers and team members, in a very different way.

Depending on what causes you choose to support and how you set up your gratitude certificates, the certificates

---

24   Courtney Hutchison and ABC News Medical Unit, "Fried Chicken for the Cure?" ABC News, Apr. 24, 2010, https://abcnews. go.com/Health/Wellness/kfc-fights-breast-cancer-fried-chicken/ story?id=10458830.

might say something like this: "Hey Scott, just wanted to say thank you so much for allowing us to serve you. We value your business. As a personal thank you for doing business with us, we would like to let you know that 35 children in Malawi have been provided with access to clean drinking water for a whole month."

How powerful is that? Imagine if one of your most valued customers received a message like that in the mail!

There are a variety of gratitude certificate templates available, showcasing different causes and messages. Certificates are fully customizable to suit your company and giving story. You can edit the contents of the certificate directly within your browser and choose to either print and mail it or send it via email.

However you decide to give back, just make sure you do it in an authentic way that aligns with your company's values, not just as a way to look good.

TIP #37
Create a Culture of Gratitude

First, understand that nobody runs a business alone. No matter how good an individual person is, it takes a team to succeed. If you want to create a culture of gratitude, realize that your team, your clients, your customers, your vendors, your coaches all have a life outside of work. This goes back to treating people with kindness and building a personal relationship.

When you're looking to build your team, start by hiring genuinely good people who will create a positive environment by treating other people well. When you have that piece in place, it's easy to build a culture around kindness and gratitude.

Your customers will stick around longer and come back more frequently. They'll spread the word to their friends. Soon, having a culture of gratitude and friendliness will become a business strategy for growth.

Tony Grebmeier is the co-owner of ShipOffers, an eight-figure business that has been an Inc. 5000 Company for the past four years in a row. I sat down with Tony as part of The Grateful Entrepreneur Summit to talk about company culture.

Tony is a big believer that everyone on the team should know a company's mission and values. If one of your values is kindness, communicate that to your team frequently so they know that kindness is a company value. Then they can make decisions and interact with others accordingly as they go about their workday. Take away the corporate stuff and simplify your values around how you want to be treated. Hire with these cultural values in mind.

Most leaders of companies only care about a team member while they're on the clock. Tony's approach is different. He has a personal buy in for each of his team member's dreams and goals. Sometimes this even means personal goals like having kids or buying a home. Tony leads by saying: "We are a stepping stone to where you want to go in life. I want to help you get to that next level." It's not about a clock in, clock out relationship. It's about shifting from the head to the heart and helping people to see themselves better than they can see themselves now.

TIP #38
Refer Customers to Your Customers

We all want our customers to help us out by referring business to us. Well, some of your customers have their own businesses. Help them out by referring potential customers to their business. What a way to show them gratitude! You can even promote events they are having, articles they've written, or anything else you think your audience will like of theirs.

For example, if one of your clients is a real estate agent, and you have a friend looking for a house, you can refer your friend to your real estate agent client. That would be a way of showing gratitude to your client.

Maybe your client is an author launching a new book. Help them out by buying a copy or spreading the word on Facebook. [Hey, I'm an author now with this book! Hint Hint!]. One of my Fit For Photos clients, Heidi Hutchinson, has authored several books. When she releases a new one, I do my best to tell my audience about it on Facebook. She sometimes does a Facebook event as a launch party and has me participate as a special guest. It's the least I could do for her, considering how supportive she's been for my business.

Maybe your client is opening a new business. Post something about it on social media, or attend their grand opening if they are local to you. My friend Carrie owns a fitness business in Florida, and recently one of her clients was having a grand opening for their new store, called the Main Ingredient. Carrie wrote a very thoughtful post on Facebook to support her client and friend:

> I'm SO excited for our dear friend and client who just opened the perfect little store called the "Main Ingredient" in Lutz/Land O'Lakes. I stopped in yesterday and the decor is so welcoming and the products she is offering are top-notch quality. You will find spices, teas, flours, oils, and more! Your cooking at home just got a whole lot better. No more boring chicken for dinner.
>
> Christina Maria Ferraro Sweet will help you pick the perfect seasoning, oil, and tea for your desired tasting. She has spent 2 years educating herself on all the products so not only can she offer you the quality products, but she can share with you how to use them.

So many times we skip making a new recipe because we don't know what to do with the ingredients after.

Another thing I love is she offers different sizes for the oils and bulk options for the teas, raw nuts, different flours, spices; so no more waste!

I highly recommend you check it out. She is having a "Grand Opening" tomorrow (Friday) 4pm–8pm, with raffles, food tasting, music and some give back to a charity near and dear to her.

I'm SO proud of her and her new venture. It is definitely a needed service and products to help us make cooking easier and healthier! Something in our fast-paced lives we can appreciate!

How might you funnel business toward your loyal clients and customers? Who knows how this goodwill may come back around to you?

TIP #39

Unplug and Create Space

I've been talking about the concept of unplugging for a while now.

We're in an age of information overload. Our cell phones are glued to our hips or stuffed under our pillows when we sleep.

More and more studies are showing that our world has an unhealthy attachment to technology.

Joshua Becker shares seven reasons to unplug:

1. **Powering-down helps remove unhealthy feelings of jealousy, envy, and loneliness.** Researchers recently discovered that one in three people felt worse after visiting Facebook and more dissatisfied with their lives. Powering-down for a period of time provides opportunity to reset and refocus appreciation and gratitude for the lives we have been given.

2. **Powering-down combats the fear of missing out.** Scientifically speaking, the Fear of Missing Out (FOMO) has been recognized as a recently emerging psychological disorder brought on by the advance of technology. Turning off social media and finding contentment in our present space is a welcome skill.

3. **Solitude is harder to find in an always-connected world.** Solitude grounds us to the world around us. It provides the stillness and quiet required to evaluate our lives and reflect on the message in our hearts.

4. **Life, at its best, is happening right in front of you.** Our world may be changing. But the true nature of life is not. Life, at its best, is happening right in front of you. These experiences will never repeat themselves. These conversations are unfiltered and authentic. And the love is real. But if we are too busy staring down at our screen, we're gonna miss all of it.

5. **Powering-down promotes creation over consumption.** Essentially, most of our time is spent in one of two categories: consuming or creating. Certainly, technology can contribute to creating. But most of the time we spend in front of

technology is spent consuming (playing video games, browsing the Internet, watching movies, listening to music). But our world doesn't need more consuming. It needs more creating. It needs your passion, your solution, and your unique contribution. Power-down. And begin contributing to a better world because of it.

6. **Addiction can only be understood when the object is taken away.** We can never fully realize our level of addiction until the item is taken away. And the only way to truly discover technology's controlling influence on your life is to turn it off, walk away, and sense how strong the pull is to turn it back on.

7. **Life is still about flesh, blood, and eye contact.** The experience of looking another person in the eye without the filter of a screen changes everything. Each time, I am reminded that life's most fulfilling relationships are the ones in the world right in front of me. And spending too much time looking away from them does a great disadvantage to my soul and theirs.[25]

25   Adapted from Joshua Becker, "7 Important Reasons to Unplug and Find Space," becomingminimalist, accessed Aug. 24, 2018, https://www.becomingminimalist.com/unplug-please/.

Yasmin Nguyen talks about a similar concept in what he describes as taking Retirement Days.

Take a day completely for yourself and do something you love.

For Yasmin, who lives in Portland, this means driving to the Oregon Coast and enjoying the beautiful beaches. At one point in his life, Yasmin was running five different businesses at the same time: He had 10 tenants, three rental properties, a web design business, a food business and ecommerce store and a social club. Yasmin had serious FOMO (fear of missing out); he thought he could juggle everything. But he realized that it became completely overwhelming. He was sleeping in his office, his health was suffering, his relationships were failing, and he hit total burnout as a result.

Yasmin started taking weekly Retirement Days, allowing him to enjoy more connection, joy, and freedom in his life. They allowed him to step back and be grateful for what he had, which ultimately led to better health, better performance, and business growth.

For Yasmin, as a result of creating this space in his life and intentionally filling the space with what he calls life-giving experiences, he was able to gain clarity and reconnect with himself. He ended up getting rid of all of his business except one. He healed his body and developed amazing relationships.

Yasmin's Retirement Days concept is similar to the unplugged adventure trips that I (and some of my clients) go on.

It's a chance to get away from the day-to-day stress of our lives and do something for us!

When you give yourself the gift of a retirement day or unplug for a period of time, you come back feeling recharged, energized, and more creative.

You'll perform better in your business, and your clients and customers will have a better experience.

Try it out!

TIP #40

Listen to Your Customers

Listening to your customers is a great way to show you value them. It can be anything from hearing a complaint and doing something about it, to taking their suggestion on how to improve your service or an addition to your business.

I recently moved to a new apartment in Denver, and boy is the treatment I get from the new leasing office much different, and better, than my old apartment.

A great example is in my old apartment, my car got broken into in our secure parking garage—turns out it wasn't so secure. When I told the manager at the leasing office, he basically gave the standard response: "Make sure to lock your doors, and don't leave any valuables in your car." He promised they would look into possibly installing cameras in the garage. I took this to mean they weren't going to do anything about it. Keep in mind that my car wasn't the only one to get broken into. There was one night that more than 10 cars were broken into, so this was a recurring problem.

Contrast that with the next apartment I lived in, Alexan Uptown, where the entrance to the parking garage was broken for several weeks. Their solution? They hired a security guard to man the garage from 6 p.m. to 6 a.m. Every time a resident entered the garage during those hours, they had to give the guard their name and apartment number, waiting while the guard compared that information with resident records. Can you see how my new apartment took a proactive approach to solving a problem and make sure their residents felt safe?

Listen to your customers and show them you care.

EPILOGUE
YOU: The Grateful Entrepreneur

You now have all the tips and tools you need to become a grateful entrepreneur. It's nothing earth shattering. It doesn't take any special skills. You already have it inside of you. Remember the Golden Rule? Treat others as you wish to be treated. Follow that and you will be very successful with your business and your life!

Mary Kay Ash once said, "Pretend that every single person you meet has a sign around his or her neck that says, 'Make me feel important.' Not only will you succeed in sales, you will succeed in life."[26]

Business comes down to building relationships. Treat people with kindness. Care about them. Listen to them. Make them feel valued and important.

---

26 "Mary Kay Ash Quotes," BrainyQuote, accessed Aug. 24, 2018, https://www.brainyquote.com/quotes/mary_kay_ash_175250.

And if you need some direction about where to start, take out a card and a pen, and write "Dear ..."

Bibliography

Bean, Travis. "A Thank You Card that Stands out from the Crowd." Ratchet + Wrench. Dec. 7, 2017. https://www.ratchetandwrench.com/articles/5348-a-thank you-card-that-stands-out-from-the-crowd.

Becker, Joshua. "7 Important Reasons to Unplug and Find Space." becomingminimalist. Accessed Aug. 24, 2018. https://www.becomingminimalist.com/unplug-please/.

Bhattacharyya, Suman. "Send flowers: How banks are wooing customers with personal gifts." Tearsheet. July 20, 2017. http://www.tearsheet.co/modern-banking-experience/send-flowers-how-banks-are-wooing-customers-with-personal-gifts.

Conner, Cheryl. "How Gratitude Advances Marketing and Business." Forbes. Apr. 26, 2017. https://www.forbes.com/sites/cherylsnappconner/2017/04/26/how-gratitude-advances-marketing-and-business/ - 5d35c0f37d68.

"Customer Service Tips: Build Customers for Life."
Accessed August 14, 2018. http://debbieelbrecht.com/
uploads/3/4/6/9/34697515/customer_service_tips.pdf.

Fairchild, Caroline. "Zappos' 10-Hour Long Customer
Service Call Sets Record." HuffPost. Updated Dec. 21,
2012. https://www.huffingtonpost.com/2012/12/21/
zappos-10-hour-call_n_2345467.html.

Fowler, Geoffrey. "Want better customer service? Don't
call. Text." *Washington Post*. Aug. 9, 2018. https://
www.washingtonpost.com/technology/2018/08/09/
want-better-customer-service-dont-call-text/?utm_
term=.2908f64e98c7.

Help Scout. "25 Ways to Thank Your Customers." Accessed
Aug. 21, 2018. https://www.helpscout.net/25-ways-to-
thank your-customers/.

"How one simple idea nurtures referrals year in
and year out." Gratitude Marketing. Sept. 27,
2016. https://gratitudemarketingbook.com/
one-simple-idea-nurtures-referrals-year-year/.

Hutchison, Courtney and ABC News Medical Unit.
"Fried Chicken for the Cure?" ABC News.
Apr. 24, 2010. https://abcnews.go.com/Health/
Wellness/kfc-fights-breast-cancer-fried-chicken/
story?id=10458830.

Isaacs, Florence. "How to Write a Condolence Note to a Customer or Client." Legacy connect. May 17, 2013. http://connect.legacy.com/profiles/blogs/how-to-write-a-condolence-note-to-a-customer-or-client.

Marie, Jenna. "What to Write in Business Sympathy Cards." Simple Sympathy. Aug. 11, 2013. http://simplesympathy.com/business-sympathy-cards.html.

"Mary Kay Ash Quotes." BrainyQuote. Accessed Aug. 24, 2018. https://www.brainyquote.com/quotes/mary_kay_ash_175250.

"Maya Angelou Quotes." Goodreads. Accessed August 22, 2018. https://www.goodreads.com/quotes/5934-i-ve-learned-that-people-will-forget-what-you-said-people.

Pinsker, Joe. "The Psychology Behind Costco's Free Samples." *The Atlantic*. Oct. 1, 2014. https://www.theatlantic.com/business/archive/2014/10/the-psychology-behind-costcos-free-samples/380969/.

Poore, Jake. "Showing Kindness and Gratitude in a Team Meeting—Here's How We Do It." Accessed Aug. 24, 2018. https://www.wecreateloyalty.com/how-to-show-kindness-in-team-meetings/.

Prieto, Julia. "How We Leverage Gratitude to Drive a Business Model." The DonorsChoose Blog. Nov. 24, 2015. https://www.donorschoose.org/blog/power-of-student-thank you-notes/.

Sant, Tom. *The Giants of Sales*. New York: AMACOM, 2006.

Silver, Yanik. *Evolved Enterprise*. Ideapress Publishing, 2017.

University of Utah. "Nature nurtures creativity." EurekAlert! Dec. 12, 2012. https://www.eurekalert.org/pub_releases/2012-12/uou-nnc120712.php.

Weller, Chris. "A CEO who writes 8,000 employee birthday cards a year just got the ultimate 'thank you'." Business Insider. Jan. 18, 2018. http://www.businessinsider.com/ceo-writes-8000-birthday-cards-a-year-gets-ultimate-thank you-2018-1.

Zwiebach, Elliot. "Marsh increases in-store sampling." Supermarket News. Feb. 28, 2005. https://www.supermarketnews.com/archive/marsh-increases-store-sampling.

Acknowledgments

I've learned a lot over my lifetime and have many people to be grateful for. Thank you, Lori Heisler, for encouraging me to take that trip to Guatemala, for always helping me be a better person, and for reminding me to celebrate my wins.

Thank you to Pat Rigsby for being my business coach for over a decade and for suggesting (over and over again) that I write a book.

Thanks to Steve Scott, who was there answering my questions about the process of writing a book.

Thank you to the amazing people at Hug It Forward for the opportunity to go to Guatemala, to learn about their culture, and to help build schools.

Thank you to my incredible editing and design team at Archangel Ink: Kristie, Paige, Jordan, and Rob.

And last but not least, a thank you to my parents, Jim and Gloria, along with my brother and sister, Chris and

Jill. Each of them played a role in shaping me to be the person I am today, and they have been supportive through my entire entrepreneurial career.

I really appreciate everyone that participated in The Grateful Entrepreneur Summit and allowed me to interview them.

Bonus Materials

You've read about The Grateful Entrepreneur Summit many times in this book, and now I'm excited to be able to share the full-length interviews with you. They represent so much wisdom, hard work, and passion cultivated by amazing entrepreneurs.

You can download all the interviews mentioned in this book at https://sayitwithgratitude.com/bonuses.

And don't forget to check out the good work they're doing:

Yasmin Nguyen; http://joyfullivingproject.com

Yanik Silver: https://evolvedenterprise.com

Pat Rigsby: https://patrigsby.com

Holly Rigsby: http://hollyjoirigsby.com

Dr. Paul White: http://www.appreciationatwork.com

Doug Spurling: http://dspurling.com

Honorée Corder: http://honoreecorder.com

John Ruhlin: http://giftologybook.com

Stephanie Jones: http://givinggal.com

Tony Grebmeier: http://tonygrebmeier.com

Erik Rokeach: http://socialproofconsulting.com

Alicia Streger: http://fitproessentials.com

David Frey: https://www.willpowersecret.com

Nae Morris: https://www.wufoo.com

Curtis Lewsey: http://www.appreciationmarketing.com

Mike Carrillo: http://fetchrev.com

Jack Blenkinsopp: https://www.b1g1.com

Steven Littlefield: https://stevenalittlefield.com

Mike Sciortino: http://gratitudemarketingbook.com

About the Author

Scott Colby is a lover of adventure who has created businesses around his passions. Although he has spent over a decade in the fitness industry helping people create physical transformations, it is his love of international travel and thirst for adventure and a better world that led him to create his newest company, Say It With Gratitude.

Scott currently lives in Denver, Colorado. When he's not writing thank you cards, he enjoys hiking, kayaking, whitewater rafting, traveling, playing with his cats, Nomar and Mia, and drinking his daily café au lait.

Made in the USA
Lexington, KY
27 September 2018